PRAISE FOR
THE FEARLESS FACILITATOR
by
Paul Maltby

"I have shared the stage with Paul, and I learn something new every time I do. It's great that he is now sharing his straight-forward, clear, practical advice with everyone. Paul's willingness to share his own triumphs and disasters offers a refreshing insight into the world of top-level facilitation."
—Perry Holley, Managing Partner, The Remarkable Manager®, and author of *Repeat the Remarkable*

"Perhaps more than ever, the world needs people who can harness the wisdom and power of groups. But working with groups can be difficult, particularly when you're new to it. With *The Fearless Facilitator,* Paul has done something really helpful – condensing years of experience into an easy-to-read 'handbook'. By weaving together stories and top tips, he has created a valuable resource for anyone wanting to improve their skills and gain confidence."
—Andrew Jackson, CEO, ProReal Ltd

"Paul has written a must-read for anyone who desires to improve their facilitation skills and leave their audience feeling like they made a wise decision to invest their precious time. As a bonus, you will have more confidence and find joy in facilitating again."
—Mary Guirovich, CEO, My Promotion Plan

"Paul is a highly skilled facilitator who adeptly enables audiences at all levels to progress their learning journeys. In this book he provides straightforward, easy-to-remember frameworks and tips to show you how to become a fearless facilitator and have fun!"
—Suzanne McGovern, Chief Diversity Officer, Splunk

"Having facilitated executive teams and large events for some of the world's most recognized organizations for 17 years, one can fall into a comfort zone that there is not too much more to learn. Over the last 4 years, I've had the opportunity to co-facilitate several times with Paul and have benefitted immensely from observing and learning from Paul's approach to creating and facilitating superb workshops and learning events. Having now read *The Fearless Facilitator*, it's clear to see that it offers one of the most comprehensive and valuable additions to the genre of professional facilitation. Describing this book as good value would be a huge underestimation; it's like eating at a Michelin star restaurant, but only being asked to pay the price of a takeaway pizza. If you're serious about upping your game in the world of facilitation and training, this has to be the one to read."
—Alec Grimsley, Executive team coach, facilitator and bestselling author of *Vital Conversations*

"Whether you've spent a lifetime facilitating or you are just planning your first work, *The Fearless Facilitator* has something for everyone – a great practical guide."
—Simon Thomson, Director, Steps Drama

THE FEARLESS FACILITATOR

THE FEARLESS FACILITATOR

A PROVEN PLAN FOR LEADING SUCCESSFUL MEETINGS, DYNAMIC WORKSHOPS, AND EFFECTIVE TRAINING EVENTS

PAUL MALTBY

The Fearless Facilitator © 2021 by Paul Maltby. All rights reserved.

Published by Author Academy Elite
PO Box 43, Powell, OH 43065
www.AuthorAcademyElite.com

All rights reserved. This book contains material protected under International and Federal Copyright Laws and Treaties. Any unauthorized reprint or use of this material is prohibited. No part of this book may be reproduced or transmitted in any form or by any means, electronic or mechanical, including photocopying, recording, or by any information storage and retrieval system, without express written permission from the author.

Identifiers:
Library of Congress Control Number: 2020912851
ISBN: 978-1-64746-385-4 (paperback)
ISBN: 978-1-64746-386-1 (hardback)
ISBN: 978-1-64746-387-8 (ebook)

Available in paperback, hardback, e-book, and audiobook

Any Internet addresses (websites, blogs, etc.) and telephone numbers printed in this book are offered as a resource. They are not intended in any way to be or imply an endorsement by Author Academy Elite, nor does Author Academy Elite vouch for the content of these sites and numbers for the life of this book.

Some names and identifying details have been changed to protect the privacy of individuals.

To Emma, Thomas and Poppy, my true north.

Contents

Introduction: Help! 1

PART I – THE ICEBERG

Chapter 1: Purpose 9

Chapter 2: Resilience. 20

Chapter 3: Environment 36

Chapter 4: Venue. 49

Chapter 5: Engagement 69

Chapter 6: Needs. 84

Chapter 7: Team 97

PART II – THE SHIELD

Chapter 8: S – Specify............................119

Chapter 9: H – Hand back the question.............124

Chapter 10: I – Involve the rest of the group.........128

Chapter 11: E – Evolve the question................133

Chapter 12: L – Look or Leave.....................146

Chapter 13: D – Distract them with something different..152

PART III – THE SWAN

Chapter 14: Think Before Acting...................164

Chapter 15: Green Intervention Strategies...........177

Chapter 16: Amber Intervention Strategies..........192

Chapter 17: Red Intervention Strategies.............204

Epilogue..223

Notes...225

Index...231

PREFACE

I have spent the last twenty years running external client and internal employee workshops, meetings, and training sessions. During that time, I've encountered all kinds of challenging situations. I've led some fantastic events where everything went according to plan. I've also led events that didn't go so well. Either way, I've learned valuable lessons and share them within this book.

Bringing people together can be expensive, so it needs to be worth the time, effort, and money. It can be frustrating for everyone involved when an event fails to deliver value to those attending. The stakes are high!

There's a lot to manage when leading an event. The group needs you to guide them through a process to reach a specific goal. At the same time, you need to manage the group dynamics and build relationships among the participants to foster collaboration and cooperation. The potential for unexpected problems to occur and derail an event is vast.

I wanted to share the proven plan I follow, which helps me prevent or mitigate challenging situations at events. I also wanted to share my tips and techniques for dealing with difficult questions and behaviors. You never know what people will say or do during an event. Being able to access helpful strategies to deal with such uncertainty has helped me many times.

All the above has led me to write this book. I aim to help as many people as possible to avoid the mistakes I've made. I want others to benefit from my learning and accelerate their success in leading events.

ACKNOWLEDGEMENTS

First and foremost, special thanks are due to Alex Davies Codina, Anouk van Batenburg, Benedikt Loser, Chris Hurd-Wood, Geoff Foster, Guy Stephens, Keith Burgess, Kris Kleist, Julia Francis, Justin Douglas, Markus Humcke, Mihai Nastasescu, Richard Rudman, Scott Summers, Stephen Thelwell, Susanne Secher, and Wendy Lim. All these people are amazing facilitators. Watching them in action over the years has taught me so much. While each of these people has a very different facilitation style, their ability to inspire others has been the same over the years. Together, they have touched thousands of lives, making a difference to people every week. I am both proud and privileged to know these people and to have spent time working with them.

I want to thank my wife, Emma, and my children, Thomas, and Poppy, who have all been incredibly supportive and patient throughout the process of writing this book.

Poppy's enthusiasm for the project led her to design many beautiful book covers. I also want to thank Bethany Wykes, the inspiration behind the cover design.

I want to give a special thanks to my endorsers. Each of them took the time and effort to read the book before publication and support it through their endorsement.

I want to thank Chris Smith and Christian Simpson for inspiring me to write this book. They are both authors and trusted advisors.

Finally, I would like to thank Kary Oberbrunner and his team at Author Academy Elite, who have been incredible partners, supporting me through the publishing process. I have learned so much.

INTRODUCTION

HELP!

I arrived full of confidence at the IBM Frankfurt office on a cold and dank Monday afternoon. A seasoned facilitator, I was preparing to run a two-day event for twenty-four Project Managers that would focus on how to build effective relationships. My co-facilitator and I had been allocated a large conference room with natural light and moveable tables. As a bonus, the rest of the building was empty, which meant no one would hijack our valuable space, which was always a risk when running events in the office. It was a great start.

While waiting for my co-facilitator to arrive, I started preparing the room. I rearranged the furniture to the desired layout and began drawing up some of the flip charts needed. The two items I was very keen on locating were the handouts and a projector, neither of which appeared to be in the room. I assumed they were in the printing office in the main building, which had been the case the last time I ran an event at the IBM Frankfurt Office. I was unable to verify this because the printing office had already closed for the day. I would have to wait until the next morning to check.

My co-facilitator, Pat, arrived around 6 p.m. We finished our flip charts, some of which we hung up to add some color and intrigue to the room when our group arrived the next day. We ran through the schedule to check we both knew what we were doing before heading off to the hotel. The fact that we hadn't managed to find the handouts bothered us. Over the two days of the program, there were many handouts, and they would take time to sort. We convinced ourselves we could cope, even if it meant sorting them as we went along.

We arrived at the office around 7.45 a.m. the next morning. We went straight to our conference room and immediately realized something was wrong. The office cleaners had done a thorough job overnight. Not only had they removed all the flips we'd diligently hung on the walls, but they had also removed all the prepared flips hiding within the flip chart stands. Everything was gone! Two hours of preparation wasted. We both felt annoyed, frustrated, and sad that so much good work was lost. To regain some composure, I left Pat to redraw some critical flips while I went to find our missing items. I managed to secure a projector, but there was no sign of the handouts. We had no printing.

I suddenly felt a strange sensation in my stomach, like the feeling you get when you get to the airport for an international flight, and you realize you've forgotten your passport. Even though the weather was cold, I began to sweat. With less than an hour before the start of the event, our participants would start arriving soon, and we had no flipcharts and no printing.

I rushed back to the conference room. I broke the news to Pat, who had at least done the flips we would need to kick off the event. All was not lost. I usually carry spare hard copies of the handouts needed for each event, and this event was no exception. There was a printer room close by, one key benefit of being in the office. When I got to the copier, it was flashing an error message in German. There was no helpful diagram showing what was wrong, only a small control panel with the error message. There was no one around to ask for help. To make matters worse, we couldn't even get our laptops connected to the local Wi-Fi to send fresh printing to the printer and bypass the copier.

Time was ticking away, and we had only thirty minutes to go before the planned start time of 9 a.m. Our pulse rates were rapidly increasing as participants began to arrive and cautiously wandered in to check if they were in the right room. Instead of the planned, calm, and confident meet and greet, all they got was a quick, "Hello. We're having some technical issues; please take a seat."

Our numerous attempts at resolving our printing problem had failed, and we were getting desperate. Our one success was that we had managed to get the projector working, so as a last resort, we could drive the event using slides.

I dispatched Pat to find another copier and sort out the printing. With around ten minutes to go, we had a full class wondering who we were. We had been running around like headless chickens ever since they arrived and had failed to welcome them properly.

Pat managed to get the handouts copied, so we had our printing—finally. We ended up using more slides than planned to compensate for the missing flipcharts, and we facilitated the event without further incident. However, our event had hardly begun, and we were already physically and mentally drained with the strain of trying to resolve all the problems.

The moral of the story is that what can go wrong often does. The more prepared you are, the easier it will be to deal with challenging situations as they arise. Many problems occur before the event has even started. Those who run events are often fearful of what might go wrong and cannot deal with unexpected issues. This book will provide you with a proven plan, tips, and techniques to become fearless by enabling you to do two things:

1. Avoid or mitigate as many challenging situations as possible by following a structured planning and preparation process

2. Have the confidence and belief to deal with anything that happens successfully and without fuss

The book consists of three parts with my Frankfurt experience inspiring the first part, called "The Iceberg." It includes seven key areas to address, either before or at the start of an event, to help you avoid as many challenging situations as possible.

The seven areas form the PREVENT checklist. The Iceberg represents the effort required by a facilitator to prepare and run an event. A more significant investment in planning and preparation can result in fewer problems occurring during the event. At the same time, the group will only see a small proportion of a facilitator's overall effort. Each element of the PREVENT checklist has a dedicated chapter that explains it in-depth and covers the benefits of investing time and effort in each item and what typical challenging situations you can avoid. There will also be some top tips to help further reduce the chances of a challenging situation occurring.

Part Two is called "The Shield" and is devoted to dealing with difficult questions. It can be challenging enough to facilitate an event full of intelligent, busy individuals and help them achieve an outcome. Dealing with difficult questions can make it more challenging. Questions can throw you off course, potentially derailing the event. They can impact your confidence and credibility. You may look like a deer staring

INTRODUCTION

into an oncoming car's headlights if you cannot deal with a question effectively.

Part Two covers six strategies that you can deploy to defend yourself when dealing with difficult questions, known as the SHIELD strategies. The SHIELD will help maintain the relationship between you and the group while helping them find their answers. Each approach has a dedicated chapter and will use specific examples to illustrate how you can deploy the strategy calmly and confidently. Sometimes, there may be more than one strategy required. If so, you can follow the SHIELD strategies in sequence (they can be used in isolation too).

Part Three focuses on how to handle challenging behaviors during an event. People who have conquered their fear of public speaking can often remain petrified at the uncertainty of challenging behaviors and how to deal with them. I have felt such pain, and that is the inspiration behind Part Three. When I run Train-the-Trainer events, the module on "How to handle challenging behaviors" is the most eagerly-anticipated one. It has been the case every time I've presented over the last twenty years.

During my time as a facilitator, I have encountered many challenging behaviors. I will cover the more common ones in Part Three, what I call "The Swan." When trying to handle challenging behavior, you will be trying to remain calm and confident on the surface while working hard underneath, like a swan. You may look calm, but your mind is racing, trying to analyze what is going on to determine how best to address the behavior.

Part Three offers a helpful set of questions to determine what might be going on to help you decide the best course of action. It then goes on to describe a range of interventions that you can employ. There are three severity levels available to address challenging behavior (Green, Amber, and Red). Each level has a dedicated chapter explaining how to use the strategies within it, and it will also cover what typical behaviors each intervention could address.

At whom is this book aimed?

The book aims to help anyone who wants to run successful events. The types of events the book can help with include:

- Meetings
- Workshops
- Mastermind groups
- Lunch and learn sessions
- Training events

The techniques and strategies covered in this book can help those who want to improve how they plan and run their events. While the book is written with face-to-face events in mind, most of the ideas, tips, and techniques will also work for those people wanting to run successful, virtual events.

Well-designed and well-run events can increase the chances of success and reduce challenging situations and behaviors. This book will help those who want both themselves and their group to look forward to an event rather than dread it.

You don't have to read the whole book to get value. It can be used as a reference guide to tackle specific areas of concern and offer suggestions to address those subjects. However, reading the whole book will provide you with strategies and techniques that will enhance your confidence and success when planning and running an event.

PART I
THE ICEBERG

CHAPTER 1

PURPOSE

Why are we here, and what are we trying to achieve?

Some years ago, I delivered Consulting skills courses for junior consultants. It helped to prepare them for their client delivery projects. They learned how to:

- Conduct interviews
- Run workshops
- Present recommendations
- Build client relationships
- Run a small project

Part of the course was a case study where four trainers role-played different clients with different personalities, roles, and responsibilities. The case study company was losing money, and the junior consultants needed to identify the cause of the losses and recommend solutions. To start, the consultants interviewed each client to gather information on what might be happening. They then ran a workshop with the clients to clarify the problem further.

The interview purpose was usually explained to the clients clearly. However, when it came to the workshop, agreeing on the purpose ahead of the exercise tended to cause problems for everyone. Most of the time, the students were eager to find a solution and used the workshop to explore solutions with their clients rather than focus on understanding the problem further.

Not having received any briefing from their consultants, the clients had no clue what to expect in the workshop. They were surprised when the consultants revealed that the purpose of the workshop was to discuss solutions to stem their losses. Two clients usually reacted to this surprise with objections.

"How can we possibly consider solutions when we don't fully understand where the losses are coming from?"

"How do we know the solutions will fix the problem?"

The other two clients reacted passively to see how the consultants would handle their muted reaction. They would disengage from the workshop, saying very little, showing subtle signs of frustration and disappointment.

The students had a choice—either listen to the clients and change the workshop's purpose to focus on the client's need or carry on as planned?

For those teams who adapted the purpose to meet the client's needs, the rest of the workshop went very smoothly. They made progress in understanding the root cause of the problem. For the teams who stuck to the plan and focused on solutions, the remainder of the workshop went less well. The session felt like a presentation of solutions rather than an interactive workshop. With no clear understanding of the root cause of the losses, the clients struggled to see which solution would be useful.

The learning de-brief of the workshop centered around the purpose and how it differed between what the clients and the consultants were expecting. The students realized that the expectations of the workshop weren't tested with their clients beforehand. The workshop failed largely due to the mismanagement of expectations and the inability of the students to adapt to the needs of their clients. The students learned that having a clear purpose isn't enough; it must also align with the attendees' expectations. Ultimately, they discovered the value of getting the purpose right for an event and how challenging it can be when it's wrong.

This chapter will look at the value of getting the purpose right. Challenging situations will occur if it isn't right, and your group will struggle to see the value of the event and them being there.

Three questions to determine the purpose of an event

During my twenty years of designing and running events, I have learned that defining the purpose is critical. It should be priority number one. Determining what the session is trying to achieve will take time and effort, and it will feel counter-intuitive because of the pressure to plan the event. However, it will be time well spent because knowing the purpose will shape the rest of the planning process. If it's your event, the onus is on you to figure out the "why." If you're running a session for someone else, work with them to define the purpose. The new, junior consultants didn't invest time in shaping their workshop purpose with their clients and experienced resistance because of it. There are three crucial questions to ask yourself or your sponsor to plan an event.

1. Is an event necessary?
2. Is everyone aligned on the purpose and outcome?
3. Whom do you need to achieve the outcome?

1. Is an event necessary?

In today's business world, people's schedules are full of meetings; there are even meetings to plan other meetings. Before adding one more appointment into their diaries, consider if the purpose warrants an event. There may be another way of achieving the outcome. For instance, if there's a need to gather opinions on a topic, that could be more efficiently obtained through a survey or questionnaire.

If the purpose is to share information, there are many software-collaboration tools available, e.g., Slack, Trello, Mural. Team members can contribute to one shared forum and allow everyone to see all submitted entries. They can also comment and post questions against contributions. Such functionality is particularly valuable if the team is virtual, dispersed, or operating in different time zones. You will prevent your group from feeling aggrieved by having to attend a meeting late at night or very early in the morning.

If the purpose is to make a simple decision, one alternative would be to run a poll where respondents could vote for the best option.

TOP TIP

Do not assume you need to run an event. Let the purpose guide you to the best way of achieving the desired outcome.

2. Is everyone aligned on the purpose and outcome?

People typically come together to achieve what individuals cannot do alone. For example, to hold discussions, solve problems, resolve conflict, strengthen relationships, or achieve buy-in when making decisions. The aim of the facilitator is to harness the collective strengths of the participants to achieve the desired outcome required. Whatever the reason for holding an event, ensure you have clarity on purpose and outcome. We'll use Problem Solving as a worked example. Solving problems can be broken down into three key stages:

1. Defining the problem
2. Identifying possible solutions
3. Determining an action plan to implement the agreed solution

There can be a different purpose for each stage. As the facilitator, the critical question is, "How will you (and your group) know when you've achieved the purpose, and the event has been a success?"

Regardless of which stage you're starting at, ensure the outcome aligns with the purpose by including two key ingredients:

a) Desired outcome—What's your measurable output?

b) Agreement—What agreement is needed to confirm your outcome?

Example: Defining the source of the problem.
Purpose: To identify why the Company is losing money.
Desired outcome: The cause of the loss is understood, and

Agreement:	Everyone agrees with the conclusions made and what next steps to take.

There would be similar statements defining the solutions and action planning stages of problem-solving. The three steps could all be done in one event, depending on the size of the problem. For example:

Purpose:	To identify why the Company is losing money, identify options to prevent further losses, and agree on a way forward.
Desired outcome:	The root cause of the problem is understood, appropriate solutions found, and
Agreement:	Everyone agrees with the actions to implement the solutions.

Being able to combine all three stages may depend on the availability of the people and time needed. If the problem is complex and more time is required to get to the desired outcome, consider breaking each stage down into three separate events.

It will be helpful for everyone to have clarity on why the event is necessary (purpose), what everyone is working towards (desired outcome), and what is required to reach the desired outcome (agreement).

TOP TIP

Ensure the agreed purpose and desired outcome are visible throughout the event using a flip chart or handout as a reference point. It will help prevent folks from drifting away from the agreed purpose and outcome. If possible, get agreement from the stakeholders beforehand

PURPOSE

to avoid wasting time clarifying and adjusting them at the event. Managing expectations is key to preventing resistance during the event.

3. Whom do you need to achieve the outcome?

If an event is necessary and the purpose and outcome are defined, the next question is, whom do you need to achieve the outcome? It will help to think about:

- How will each person benefit from being there?
- How will each person's presence benefit the group?

Everyone

The more people you have at an event, the more diverse views there will be. While this is a good thing, it will take more time to cover a topic.

If it requires all the team to attend to ensure that everyone's had an input to the problem or decision, then include them. Keep in mind that the people in the room should be adding value to the event. If not, they should not be there. Be clear about what you expect. If the numbers become too big to include everyone, consider asking teams to nominate and send representatives instead.

> *TOP TIP*
>
> *If there are lots of people, aim to build in more activities at the event where people work in smaller groups to increase overall participation. If everyone feels they have contributed, then overall acceptance of the outcome will increase.*

Include the Leader?

I've facilitated team events where the purpose was to understand how the team was feeling and help boost team morale. In one example, Rachel, a Team Leader, wanted me to run a session for her team. The problem was that Rachel wished to join the event to hear what her team had to say. I spent time with Rachel reviewing the team's low engagement survey scores and listening to her perspective. It looked like Rachel was causing some of the issues, so I recommended she stay out of the room. The team could potentially be reluctant to speak openly in front of Rachel about their problems and feelings.

Asking a leader not to be present can be a hard message to deliver, so tread carefully and discuss the matter with the leader in a respectful and empathetic manner. If the leader is in the room, the team will often say what they think the leader wants to hear as opposed to what they think and feel. Preventing the truth from surfacing can put the achievement of the desired outcome in jeopardy. The group's willingness to speak openly with their leader will depend on the level of psychological safety between them. If the team feels safe to engage in open dialogue in front of the leader, it may be helpful to include him/her. If the team is fearful of speaking the truth about how they feel and see things, more work will be needed to develop a climate of safety. Excluding the leader initially may be more appropriate, depending on the purpose of the event. Chapter 3 – Environment will cover how to build a safe climate with the group.

Some events will require the leader to be present to help drive thinking since the team may not feel comfortable

> The group's willingness to speak openly with their leader will depend on the level of psychological safety between them.

making decisions without leadership input. For instance, when running strategy and planning events, the leader often has insights that their team may not be aware of and which can help inform their thinking. The event purpose will shape whether it's a good idea to include the leader or not.

Who's not in the room?

Have you ever been in a meeting or workshop where the group reached an impasse because a key person was missing? Either there was a decision to be taken or vital input was needed from the absent person. How frustrating is that?

Informal influencing relationships in organizations can make the selection of participants challenging. Some individuals in an organization may be lower down the formal hierarchy but exert influence on those above them. They influence either through a more dominant personality or through their expertise. These informal hierarchies are difficult to identify on paper. Trying to work out who should support an event will more accurately be determined by talking to the sponsor and understanding the group dynamics.

For example, I facilitated a series of workshops for a client, and the leader would not decide anything unless his Technical Advisor was present. He wanted to know that his decisions wouldn't compromise the proposed technical solution. If the advisor wasn't available, I knew there was no point in scheduling the workshop. The leader wasn't afraid of making tough decisions, but he didn't have a technical background. He knew that was his blind spot and wanted the advisor present to ensure he had the right advice before making any decisions.

Event success can be influenced by who is in the room and who is not. Understanding the individuals' personalities and how they interact in a group situation can help prepare for an event. The absence of a critical figure or decision-maker can stifle progress. There may be two strong, opposing personalities in the room who consume valuable time slugging out their differences over a topic.

Understanding who's critical to achieving a successful outcome (and how they're likely to interact with others) will require an investment in time. The return is an increased probability of a smoother, more productive event by having the right people in the room to contribute to the outcome.

> **TOP TIP**
>
> *If you decide not to invite some stakeholders to an event, ensure you (or the sponsor) inform them and give the reason for exclusion. It will help to maintain the relationship and manage their expectations. You don't want them to find out from those invited. If they are not informed, they may choose to turn up for fear of missing out. Explain how they will receive information on the outcome of the meeting, so they remain informed. Hopefully, they will be grateful for avoiding yet another meeting.*

Typical challenging situations prevented by having a clear purpose

Is the event necessary?

- Disengaged hostages who don't want to be there
- Angry or disengaged stakeholders who feel they're wasting their time

Alignment on purpose and outcome

- Confusion as to what the event is all about

PURPOSE

- Participant resistance due to an unclear or wrong purpose
- A meandering meeting that stumbles to the end with no real outcome

People needed to achieve the purpose and outcome

- The group is unable to decide because a key stakeholder is missing
- The group fails to make progress due to a clash of personalities
- The group fails to surface real issues due to an unwelcome stakeholder being present
- The group is distracted or disrupted because some people see no value in meeting and are actively complaining

CHAPTER 2

RESILIENCE

Grow, Breathe, Move, Eat and Sleep

I was thrilled when I became a Management Consultant. I would get to travel and work with a variety of clients and project teams. Every week would be different. However, there was one sizable problem. As part of the job, I was to facilitate client workshops. Workshops were a new concept to me, so the thought of leading a room full of fee-paying clients and driving them to a result they needed, terrified me. I became incredibly nervous about how I would cope. I worried about how clients would judge me and my performance. Despite support from my Manager, my lack of experience and confidence got the better of me. My stress levels increased dramatically as each workshop drew nearer. I would lie awake at night, contemplating a whole host of different disaster scenarios, which only made things worse.

Consequently, leading up to a workshop, I was unable to sleep much. My nervousness was noticeable in the workshops. I had a wobbly voice, shaky hands, and displayed a general lack of eye contact with the group. It got so bad that I considered leaving my job and returning to accountancy to avoid running workshops. I had to do something.

As I was facing this life-changing decision, I received an email asking for volunteers to become part-time trainers. The opportunity would require presenting and facilitating workshops but to a more junior and internal audience. To me, working with our young talent felt like a safer scenario. I volunteered, got trained up, and began facilitating training events.

I learned a lot quickly by working with experienced facilitators on the training events. My confidence grew with each event, and with that came belief in myself—I could do this. As my experience grew, I began to enjoy facilitating, and eventually, I accepted a position to deliver training full-time. Since then, I've trained groups ranging from recent graduates to senior executives across the globe. I still get nervous, but I manage it by being fearless, knowing my coping strategies and facilitator techniques will help me deal with whatever situation occurs.

What makes the role challenging is that every group varies. Different people, venues, co-facilitators, contexts, and goals all contribute to the challenge. However, as a facilitator, you deploy the same set of skills to help each group achieve success. Knowing that should give you confidence.

The one thing that's helped me grow in my facilitation career is resilience—I believed I could get better. In the context of facilitating a group, resilience means being able to:

- Perform under pressure
- Take care of yourself

- Carry on with confidence rather than give up when faced with challenging situations
- Respond more positively and recover more quickly when faced with a perceived threat, which is any situation that could derail your event

In this chapter, we will look at the two main areas of resilience—mental and physical. Your mental state will influence your physical condition. Your mind and what you think will drive how you feel and, in turn, how the rest of your body reacts.

Mental Resilience

If you can improve your mental resilience when facilitating events, you will be amazing. Having strong mental resilience is the key to becoming a fearless facilitator. To understand the opportunity this can bring, I have broken mental resilience down into three areas:

- Focus
- Mindset
- Belief and confidence

Focus

When I first started facilitating, I was terrible. I quickly realized that my focus was wrong. My attention and concern were on me, not on my group. I had to stop worrying about how I came across to my group and focus on how I could help them instead. How could I deliver value to the group? Focusing on me and my nervousness consumed lots of negative energy. Focusing on how I could help others channeled my energy more positively and constructively. Knowing that I was meeting the needs of the group somehow calmed my nerves and improved my resilience. I learned it wasn't about me; it was about helping the group.

Mindset

As well as changing my focus, I also had to change the story I was telling myself from *"I'm not very good at facilitating workshops"* to *"I'm not very good at facilitating workshops yet."* That one word—yet—has made all the difference. I began to believe I could improve with effort, and I continue to do so with more experience.

When you face a challenging situation, you typically have two options—you either embrace it or run away from it. Embracing a challenge is a chance to learn and grow as an individual. Carol Dweck, in her book *Mindset, The New Psychology of Success*,[1] refers to this approach as having a Growth Mindset. People with a Growth Mindset see problems as something to be enjoyed because they offer learning opportunities.

Last year I received two opportunities to speak to hundreds of people at significant events. I usually work with groups of between six and one hundred, so I had a choice. Do I run away from these opportunities because they're too big? Do I embrace them as a chance to learn how to connect with such large groups? Of course, being fearless, I decided to accept the challenge. I was incredibly nervous at both events, especially wearing a microphone and standing on a large stage with lots of lights shining on me. I rehearsed my content delivery many times. I was confident in my design. I started each event with an engaging story to break the ice, and I included lots of interaction. Thanks to the radio microphone, I was able to leave the stage and mix among the group during each activity. I also had a support team each time to help with the room setup and run with the roving microphones when group members wanted to contribute. The sponsors were happy with the event, and I got some helpful feedback. Ultimately, I learned a lot about designing and delivering engaging sessions for large groups ranging from 250 to 400 people.

Your mindset will drive how your body reacts. If you allow your mind to see a challenging situation as a crisis, you may begin to panic. Your brain will see the crisis as a threat and protect itself by going into fight or flight mode. Your ability to access the knowledge and skills that will help you deal with the situation will disappear as your brain shuts down to protect you.

Conversely, having a positive attitude where you believe you can learn the skills to help deal with any crisis (Growth Mindset) will make you more resourceful. Your brain and body will react more positively. Your ability to focus, solve problems, and recall vital knowledge and skills will increase, enabling you to tackle whatever situation you're facing.

The Move from Panic to Resourcefulness

We can train the brain to limit the flight or fight reaction and recover more quickly when it perceives a threat. It is possible to choose a more helpful response to a crisis. We can't always control what happens around us, but we can control how we react. In their book *Altered Traits*, Daniel Goleman and Richard J. Davidson[2] talk about training your brain through mindfulness. Their research revealed that conducting daily mindfulness exercises can strengthen the connection between the prefrontal cortex and the amygdala. The prefrontal cortex is frequently associated with regulating our decision making and behavior. The

> **We can't always control what happens around us, but we can control how we react.**

amygdala is one part of the brain which is associated with looking for threats and triggers the flight or fight response. When the amygdala detects a potential threat, we can use the strengthened connection to the prefrontal cortex to notice the danger. We can then choose to override the flight or fight request from the amygdala. Being able to access the prefrontal cortex can reduce an adverse reaction and achieve quicker recovery time, thus increasing resilience. We can then choose a more helpful response that addresses the crisis instead of making things worse for the group and ourselves.

TOP TIP

Here is a simple, daily, three-minute mindfulness exercise.

Set a timer and find a quiet place where you won't be disturbed. Sit down somewhere comfortable with an upright posture. Close your eyes and breathe deeply and slowly through your nose. Focus on your breath and nothing else. Slowly inhale and slowly exhale.

If your mind wanders, notice it, and gently bring your focus back to your breath.

See notes for more helpful references on mindfulness exercises.[3,4]

For more practical advice on incorporating mindfulness into your daily routine to help improve resilience, I recommend looking at the Potential Project, founded by Rasmus Hougaard.[5]

Pause, Breathe and Think

If you find yourself about to panic, take a moment and breathe. Even better, take a deep breath, two, if needed. If you stop breathing, the inevitable will happen, but fast and shallow breathing can also signal the amygdala you're under threat. If you can pause, breathe slowly and deeply, and think, this will help you regain control and deal with the situation.

Belief and Confidence

> Whether you think you can or
> think you can't, you're right.
> ~ Henry Ford

If you believe you can't facilitate a group or deal with a challenging situation, you won't be able to do it. It will show through your voice and body language, and your group will begin to believe it too. They may perceive you as a weak facilitator who's not sure what to do next. Like a pack of hyenas, they may see you as the wounded gazelle on the savannah. The group may test your resolve with more challenging questions or behaviors, and the event will unravel quickly.

With belief comes confidence. The more confident you are and behave, the more your mind and body will reinforce that feeling in the way you appear in front of others. By looking more confident, you will ensure the group will engage with you as if you are a confident person. The increased engagement will provide the reinforcement you need to grow your confidence further. If you exude confidence, the group is more likely to feel they're in safe hands. They will have no reason to doubt your ability— unless you prove them wrong.

I once delivered a presentation to a client audience, and it was a total disaster. It was one of the worst experiences of my career. I wasn't supposed to present since it was a client-to-client event, supported by consultants acting as advisors. My client failed to show at the event. The client sponsor asked me to present on his behalf instead. He handed me a printed version of the slides from my client. Although I helped shape the presentation with my client, it was different from the one we agreed on. There were some slides in there that I didn't fully understand. My client had inserted them at the last minute, and there were no speaker notes which elaborated on the slides. I wasn't confident I could deliver the presentation with conviction as I didn't understand the new slides inserted by my client. I had no time to alter or hide the slides as they were on the laptop being used to show everyone's presentations.

I should have skipped the new slides, admitted they weren't mine, and moved on. Instead, I tried to bluff my way through them. My confidence and eye contact dropped, and my voice wobbled. Everyone in the room knew there was a problem with the messages on those few extra slides. That's when the difficult questions started to come. I didn't know the answers to any of them because they were asking about someone else's content.

> **If you don't understand or believe the messages you're delivering, it will show.**

Consequently, no one remembered any of my earlier recommendations. The focus was on the back end of my session and the uncertainty that surrounded it. I felt I let myself down and the client I was representing. I learned that if you don't understand or believe the messages you're delivering, it will show. If you don't have confidence and belief in what you're saying, why expect your group to do so?

There are other ways to build confidence before an event:

- Have a robust event design
- Rehearse your opening session
- See yourself succeeding

Confidence in the design

If you have a robust design with realistic timing, you will feel confident in delivering it. Validate and agree on the plan with your sponsor or key stakeholders. Check if any areas will be contentious or will require more time to work through with the group. Chapter 6 will cover in more detail how to work with your stakeholders on the event design.

Have a contingency plan if the time available for the event is reduced, e.g., work with your sponsor to agree on the priorities. Which topics can wait if time runs out? Also, consider alternate ways of getting to the same outcome in less time, e.g., brainstorming may be quicker for generating ideas than taking time to run a group discussion. Having a Plan B will give you confidence if timing starts to drift away from the original plan.

Confidence through rehearsing

If nothing else, rehearse your opening. Hopefully, by the time you're at the end of your opening, you will be in the flow, and any initial nerves will have dissipated. Telling a relevant story is a good way of opening an event. Stories are easy to remember, and people like stories so they will immediately engage. To remove the pressure of remembering key messages, consider using flip charts as reference points. Slides disappear at a click of a button. Putting essential statements on flip charts will help you remember.

Confidence through visualizing success

Imagine a successful event. You've met all the objectives. Everyone's happy with what they've achieved, and you've enhanced your reputation as a facilitator who can make things happen. Visualize it. Notice how that makes you feel.

By doing that, you are creating a new helpful pathway in your brain. It's a pathway that allows your inner voice to say, "*You can do this!*"

Visualizing the successful outcome beforehand will give you the confidence to walk the path to success when it's time to deliver the event.

Physical Resilience

It's one thing to be mentally resilient, but if you're physically not up to the task, you will still have a problem. It's difficult to be fearless when you're tired or hungover.

I learned this lesson very early in my facilitation career. It was my first internal training event. I was working with three other facilitators running a five-day course for a group of junior consultants. As a new facilitator, I made nearly every physical resilience mistake possible during that week. We were in a hotel venue, away from the office, and I partied hard into the early hours every night.

By the end of the week, my body's battery was empty. I had done no exercise, had little sleep, and drank far too much alcohol. My body had had enough. I was so tired that I overslept on the final day. I was woken up by the lead facilitator ringing my phone right before the course started. To make matters worse, I had to facilitate the whole morning with no breakfast and nursing a hangover. Everyone deserved more from me!

Facilitating an event can be exhausting. Being on your feet all day trying to remain one step ahead of the group can take its toll on you. You can't deliver your best performance when you're not feeling up to it, so you need to look after yourself.

You can improve your physical resilience by focusing on your sleep, what you consume, and how much you exercise.

Sleep

There's nothing quite like a good night's sleep to increase your physical and mental resilience. Your ability to cope with any challenging situation will increase when you feel sufficiently rested.

Variables associated with physical resilience, such as food, drink, and exercise, will impact your quality of sleep. According to research led by Max Hirshkowitz, Ph.D., Chair of the National Sleep Foundation Scientific Advisory Council, the recommended number of hours of sleep per night for adults (18-64 years) is between seven and nine hours.[6]

Not getting enough sleep will disrupt your natural body clock (circadian rhythm) and the time needed to restore any damage to the body, such as muscle growth or tissue repair. Sleep also allows time for the brain to consolidate the information and experiences gained during the day. The data is processed and transferred from short-term to long-term memory. According to the National Sleep Foundation, sleep triggers changes in the brain that help to solidify memories. Connections between brain cells are strengthened, improving information transfer and memory recall. If you want to recall your well-prepared plan during your event, get enough sleep.

Don't stress about your sleep

Due to a late receipt of a visa, travel delays, and other logistical problems, I once ran the first day of a three-day event on only ninety minutes of sleep; I don't recommend it. I wasn't at my best but, I was able to function, mainly on adrenalin. I was leading a group of four facilitators, so my impact on the group was diluted. I learned a valuable lesson. If I could survive on 90 minutes of sleep, I could survive on any amount of sleep, albeit for one day.

Before the sleep deprivation experience, I used to worry about getting enough sleep before an important event, which made falling asleep almost impossible. I would lie awake willing myself to fall asleep, which only made matters worse. I no longer worry, knowing that whatever happens with my sleep, I will survive. Taking the stress away enables me to fall asleep quite quickly and get the right amount of sleep needed.

Alcohol

Getting enough sleep (quantity) is one thing but getting enough quality sleep is vital for resilience. Regarding alcohol, my mantra is, if in doubt, leave it out! Over the years, I've noticed that I feel more rested on only seven hours of sleep and having had no alcohol versus having eight hours of sleep having drunk alcohol. Best practice for me is getting seven to eight hours of sleep with no alcohol.

My experience is backed up by Vicki Culpin in her book,[7] *The Business of Sleep—How Sleeping Can Transform Your Career*. Vicki states that any alcohol taken near bedtime will negatively affect your overall quality of sleep. Alcohol will help you fall asleep. Also, your quality of sleep in the first half of the night will improve. However, as your body processes and metabolizes the alcohol, your sleep quality during the second half of the night will be more disrupted. Accordingly, your overall sleep quality will reduce.

The only way you will sleep soundly with alcohol is to drink excessively, which is more than four standard drinks before bedtime. However, the danger of a hangover the next morning and overall risk to your health far outweigh any benefits gained by one good night's sleep.

Caffeine

According to the National Sleep Foundation, caffeine is a stimulant that can take effect as quickly as fifteen minutes.[8] It takes several hours for caffeine to leave the body. While it may be helpful to offer caffeine after lunch to get everyone over the post-lunch dip in energy, it's advisable to avoid caffeine close to bedtime. It will take longer to fall asleep as well as impact your overall sleep quality. I avoid caffeine after 4 p.m. to ensure my sleep is unaffected.

Water

Hydration is key to helping your brain function correctly. Your brain is comprised of between 75-85% water, so when your body is dehydrated, physical and mental capacity can reduce. Research from the Georgia Institute of Technology in Atlanta has shown that dehydration can significantly affect concentration.[9] Cognitive functions such as complex problem-solving, coordination, and attention can all be affected. When your group is concentrating for a long time, a reduction in cognitive ability could create more challenging situations. Tasks could take longer; creativity and energy levels could drop.

The amount of water needed per person per day varies depending on body weight, but a popular general rule of thumb is the "8x8" rule, which recommends drinking eight ounces of water eight times a day (2 liters per day). Make sure you and your group remain hydrated.

Exercise

Our bodies are not designed for sitting at a desk all day. Improving your physical and mental health by being more active can have a positive influence on your resilience. It can boost your self-esteem, confidence, and stamina, giving you a greater inner strength to approach challenging situations as they arise. Redistributing the blood from your bottom to your brain through physical activity will allow more oxygenated blood to enter the brain, and this will increase performance.

Physical activity, even in small amounts, can produce endorphins in our body, which helps relieve stress. Regular exercise also stimulates parts of the brain responsible for the release of chemicals, which helps improve our memory and cognition.[10]

TOP TIP

Immediately after physical activity, the brain is better at accomplishing tasks and more able to focus, so make sure you have time at lunch to get some fresh air and go for a brisk walk. Twenty minutes is ideal, but even a ten-minute brisk walk would provide you with a boost. Encourage your group to do the same.[11]

Habits

There are lots of things you can start doing to improve your resilience. If you want to make a change and sustain it, you may need to change your habits. Very often, we set ourselves targets which are over-ambitious and unrealistic. Most of the time, all we do is set ourselves up for failure and disappointment.

For example, one of my ambitions was to read more. I had bookshelves of books I had ordered and remained on the shelf unread. Two years ago, I decided to commit to reading one book per month, which I thought was a realistic target. I failed. Nothing changed until a friend told me about *Mini Habits*, a book by Stephen Guise.[12] The author describes "mini habits" as tiny goals so small that it's hard to set them any lower. It sounds counter-intuitive, but the secret is committing to that goal every day, thereby forming a new mini habit. My minimum daily goal for reading became one page a day, every day!

As I began to read one page a day, I noticed I had time to read a few more pages on most days. These were bonus pages for me since I had already achieved my daily goal of one page. Exceeding my daily target gave me a sense of achievement. The net result was that in my first year of starting this mini habit, I read over sixteen books, and I continue to average one to two books per month.

The same can apply to any new habit. Rather than committing to going to the gym three times a week for one hour, commit to doing one or two push-ups per day as Stephen Guise did. If you find yourself struggling to do the three-minute mindfulness exercise recommended earlier, try doing it for one minute every day.

Introducing small changes and doing them daily over time will compound and generate significant results.

When facilitating events now, I have introduced a new habit of going for a walk at lunch. Getting outside to stretch my legs and take in some fresh air, even if it's only for five minutes, helps to boost my energy for the afternoon session. What new habit will you start?

Typical challenging situations prevented by being more resilient

Mental Resilience

- Unhelpful levels of stress and anxiety before and during an event
- Inability to react positively to a challenging situation
- Forgetting your plan or next steps due to panic and amygdala hijack (your mind going blank during an event—stage fright)

- Participants testing you when you appear as if you're not sure what to do next

- Participants challenging you with difficult questions when you appear to lack confidence and belief in what you're saying

Physical Resilience

- Lack of sleep or poor sleep quality, resulting in higher levels of tiredness and lower energy levels. As a result, your group and event may be low energy, achieving less output

- Reduced patience and tolerance when dealing with challenging behaviors could lead to unhelpful interventions, making matters worse

- Reduced blood flow to the brain due to lack of exercise may limit your ability to tackle problems and challenging situations

- Limited ability to think and solve problems due to dehydration

- Running an event with an alcohol-induced hangover will reduce your ability to function, let alone tackle challenging situations

CHAPTER 3

ENVIRONMENT

How does it feel to be in the room?

Take a moment to reflect on the last event you attended or ran. How did it feel in the room? Did it feel safe, intimidating, draining, exciting, calm, chaotic? As the facilitator, you are responsible for shaping and managing how it feels to be in the room.

Very often, challenging behaviors surface when participants in the room don't feel safe. There are many different reasons why people don't feel safe when attending an event. It could be due to:

- Other particular people being in the room, e.g., more senior
- The uncertainty of what to expect

- Not knowing who else will be there
- A disruption to a daily working routine

Participants' worries are often the driving force behind challenging behaviors, so they should not be ignored. If it doesn't feel psychologically safe in the room, then the fear and anxiety that will reside in your group will inhibit their ability to think clearly and contribute positively to the event.

This chapter will look at what you can do to create a safe and welcoming environment for participants to enable them to do their best work at the event. There are things you can do:

1. Before the event
2. At the start of the event
3. During the event

1. Before the event

Richard Rudman, a friend of mine and a great facilitator, told me about an event he ran many years ago that illustrates the benefit of creating a safe, welcoming environment. He was due to deliver a three-hour training event for a team. Richard traveled to the team's location and had arranged early access to the training room, which he used to check that the room was clean and tidy. He also spent time hanging several flip charts around the room, such as a welcome flip, objectives, a schedule, and some thought-provoking quotations.

Richard had brought sticky notes and markers with him and ensured that each table group had sufficient resources. He had brought some audio speakers and was playing music in the background to enhance the ambiance. Each table group had a flip chart stand and paper. He was ready to receive his group.

With about twenty minutes to go, the sponsor walked into the room to introduce himself to Richard. Before doing so, the sponsor paused to take in the room and simply said, "This is going to be a great training event." The sponsor and Richard had never met. He had never seen Richard deliver any training. Richard encouraged the sponsor to hold off any judgment on the event's success until it was over. While the sponsor agreed, he shared with Richard that he was basing his confidence on the way the room looked. The room felt inviting with the colorful flips, the resources on the tables, and the calming music. It felt like his team was going to be in safe hands and set to receive a great training event.

> **People tend to feel safer when they feel like you care.**

Contrast this story with an event you've been to where the facilitator was not ready and was rushing around trying to plug in a laptop to show some slides. The room probably hasn't been touched since the last meeting. Discarded coffee cups and garbage may be strewn all over the place. The room makes you feel like you want to turn around and walk away. You also get a sense that the facilitator doesn't care about you, which can spark challenging behaviors to ignite. Some people may start to moan or complain about their environment. They may begin to doubt the facilitator's competency based on the poor state of their working conditions.

The crucial first step in taking care of the environment is to make it look and feel like you care about your group. People tend to feel safer when they feel like you care. Make it feel welcoming by:

- Tidying the room up if required
- Bringing the relevant materials with you
- Adding color to the room wherever possible to brighten it

- Putting flip charts or posters on the wall (if possible) providing points of reference and discussion

- Bringing audio speakers to play background music to add ambiance to the room. Talking about the music can sometimes break the ice before the event starts

- Ensuring you are ready to receive participants before the beginning of the event rather than being caught rushing around trying to finish off your preparations

If you have the time (and energy), engaging with participants before an event can help allay any fears or concerns they may have about the event. You can learn how they are feeling and address any anxiety or concerns they have. Engaging participants early on reassures the participants you care about them. Chapter 5 covers Engagement in detail.

TOP TIP

Some participants often arrive very early and can disrupt your preparations by wanting to engage in conversation. To avoid this, consider placing a note on the door indicating what time the door will be open for participants to walk into the room. Typically, this can be 15-20 minutes before the event start. You can then focus on getting the room (and you) ready for the event knowing you won't be interrupted.

2. At the start of the event

Create a Social Contract

One of the critical activities you can do at the beginning of an event is to agree on a social contract. Ultimately, it's how the group wants to work together during the event. Ideally, it should include some positive behaviors which if displayed, will enhance their experience. Examples of positive suggestions could be:

- One person talking at a time
- Active participation
- Give and receive feedback
- Have fun

The social contract should also include boundaries of what's unacceptable. For example, there could be an agreement not to use cellphones or laptops during the event. You won't be able to exclude every potential behavior using the social contract, but it will at least be a start. The agreement will set the tone for what's acceptable during the event.

If you treat the agreement as a living document, you can add to it as and when specific situations or behaviors occur. For example, some groups are better than others at coming-back on time from a break. For those groups where most participants come back late, I often have a quick discussion on the consequences of finishing past the stated end time if the group is regularly coming back late from breaks. If the group still wants to finish on time, then "be back on time" is often added to the social contract.

Suggestions for what to include in the social contract should come from the group. I often offer one or two ideas to kick things off, so everyone knows the sorts of things helpful to have in the contract. If I do, I will ask for their permission to add the suggestions, but the remainder should come from the group.

TOP TIP

Capture the social contract on a flip chart. Build it up as you receive suggestions, and the group agrees with them. Once complete, put the agreement on a wall where it's visible to all. The contract can be referred to when someone displays behavior that goes against it.

Participants often add confidentiality to the social contract. It's a significant contributor to building psychological safety in the group. If there's any hint that event discussions may go beyond the group, they will tend to hold back and be a lot less candid. Participation may reduce because of concerns about confidentiality, limiting the value gained from the event. Breaking confidentiality can destroy trust and confidence in a heartbeat, so maintaining this is a critical success factor in any event.

The social contract can be an excellent opportunity to influence the event environment and create psychological safety in the group. Providing suggestions such as, "There are no mistakes here, only learning opportunities," can set the right tone. If participants feel safe in a group where they know they won't be judged or punished for making a mistake, they will take more risks and be more creative.

Google's Project Aristotle conducted extensive research on what makes a highly effective team. The study cited five characteristics of such teams, with psychological safety being the primary one. Psychological safety is defined as when "Everyone feels safe in taking risks around their team members, and [knows] that they won't be embarrassed or punished for doing so."[13]

This ethos exists in high-performing teams and organizations across the world; such a culture exists in companies like WD-40.

Gerry Ridge, CEO of WD-40, says, *"We don't make mistakes. Each experience is a learning moment. We share our learning moments with one another so we can improve together. Our openness with learning moments provides us a circle of safety to innovate, learn, grow, and get it right without fear of reprisal.*"[14]

The tribal culture within WD-40 focuses on creating psychological safety within the group. When WD-40 employees feel safe, they are free to innovate and focus on their roles aligned with the company mission. Achieving this during an event is critical as you often have participants come together who may not know each other well, or at all. At an event, you only have a short amount of time to create such a safe environment.

There are specific suggestions you can make on the social contract, which will help establish psychological safety at the start of an event:

- Respect and explore others' opinions
- Listen actively (versus waiting to talk)
- Respect confidentiality
- Keep an open mind (don't judge others)

How to build psychological safety at the start of an event

When attending events, many people are initially reluctant to speak for fear of saying something "dumb" and embarrassing themselves. They will often sit back and assess the situation, analyzing who else is in the room. Such inhibitions can stifle interaction initially and hinder progress later if not addressed. A great way of accelerating safety and cooperation is to get everyone working on a simple question. It could be asking everyone to think about what should go in the social contract or about their event objective. Whatever the question, get them to follow a simple three-stage process:

1. Get them working individually in silence for a minute or two
2. Have them work in pairs or trios to articulate their thoughts with each other. Allow a further two or three minutes
3. Ask for the small groups to share their discussion highlights with the whole group

By the time you begin the group exercise, everyone will have had time to think about the question and verbalize their thoughts. Creating time and space for the group to consider and discuss their ideas can boost confidence levels by reducing any pressure they may initially feel.

This activity can also help when you have participants in the room who don't speak English as their first language and don't feel comfortable speaking English. They may feel more at ease talking to one or two other people and then getting a spokesperson in their pair or trio to report back to the larger group. Even if they don't speak to the broader group themselves, they have at least contributed to the question in stages one and two.

This type of activity helps to boost inclusivity, helping everyone feel comfortable and safe in getting involved in the group at some level.

3. During the event

Model the behavior you want to see from others. As the facilitator, everyone will look to you to set the benchmark on behavior during the event. Linking back to resilience, if you're not feeling your best or not giving your all, your group will know.

Every person will influence the overall mood within the room. As the facilitator, you're the most significant influencer of the climate. Standing at the front, you will be observed closely by everyone in the room. The spotlight is on you. If you're walking into the room in a bad mood because you're tired, hungover, or merely bored because you must run yet another workshop, it will be tough to disguise. If your group senses that you would rather not be there, they will start to feel the same, and the event may implode.

Model the behavior you want to see from others.

For example, once I ran a Customer Relationship Skills training event for a technical team. They came from across the globe, and it was the first time they had physically met as a team. I could feel the buzz of excitement. The team leader insisted he would kick-off the event to set the context for the training, which I thought would be a good start.

What a disaster! He lacked energy and enthusiasm. He spent fifteen minutes mumbling and staring at the ground with his hands in his pockets as he talked to his team. I looked around the room. I could see people thinking, *Oh my goodness, is this what the next two days will be like?* I've never seen the climate of a room change from positive to negative so quickly. By the time the leader had finished fifteen minutes later, the group had slumped into their chairs. The leader had no idea of his impact.

He handed the floor over to me. I changed my plan and started with a relationship-building icebreaker (see Chapter 5 - Engagement) to get the energy and enthusiasm back up quickly. There's no way I could have started the event as initially planned with the group on their knees emotionally.

Your behavior should be appropriate to the context of the event. For example, being happy and super enthusiastic when you're facilitating a workshop on how to make cuts in an organization where job losses are likely may not be appropriate. Similarly, adopting an attitude and behavior which suggests an organization is doomed, and the situation is hopeless is equally inappropriate. Whatever your behavior, it will usually be infectious.

If you want energy and enthusiasm from the group, you will need to inject it into the room.

Notice the energy in the room

As the facilitator, there's a lot to manage. You're there to support the group and guide them through the process to achieve an outcome. You're also watching the time and potentially dealing with difficult individuals. What often gets overlooked is noticing the overall energy in the room. Taking a step back and reflecting on how it feels in the room can be helpful.

- Is there still energy and enthusiasm?
- What's the noise level like when an activity is being run?
- What kind of facial expressions are you noticing?
- Are there any apparent trends in body language amongst the group?
- Are the participants still asking lots of questions, or have they switched off?
- Is there a table group or section of the room that has given up while others are beavering away?

If you notice a problem with the energy, there are a few things you can do.

Ask them

The easiest thing to do is to ask the group how they are feeling. Qualifying the reason for checking in with them can help. For example, "I'm noticing that very few people are contributing to this discussion. Can I check how people are feeling about this topic?"

There could be many reasons why only a few people are contributing to a discussion. You won't know unless you ask the group. For example, the group may need a break, or maybe some feel frustrated that they don't know enough about the topic to participate. Noticing what's going on is the first challenge. Having the courage to call it out and discuss it with the group is the next challenge.

Climate Thermometer

Another option is to use a team climate thermometer. It can be a simple scale from zero to ten about how happy people feel about the event. Zero can represent *get me out of here* with ten representing *this is the best event ever* with a sliding scale in between. You can check the scores throughout the event, at the start or at the end of key sessions. The group can call out their score or mark it on a chart.

Mad, Sad, Glad

I've also used the *Mad, Sad, Glad* technique. Write the three emotions in separate columns on a flip chart. After each section of an event, ask the group how they're feeling. They reflect on what's driving that emotion, and then they place a sticky note against the one they're feeling.

You can then see where the group's underlying mood is by looking at where the sticky notes are. You can have a short discussion on what's driving the emotion and any required changes needed to improve their experience. You can also see what's working well for the group.

Honor the social contract

When challenging behaviors arise during the event, use the social contract to help reinforce acceptable behavior. The social contract should be a great reference to remind everyone about what's acceptable behavior and what isn't. If it's not used during the event to manage challenging behaviors, you will have wasted time creating a pointless contract. You will also struggle to manage challenging behaviors. It will be similar to the parent who threatens their child with punishment but doesn't carry out the threat. The participants will quickly realize the social contract is meaningless. The participants won't respect the agreement and potentially won't respect you for not honoring it.

Don't underestimate the value placed on the contract by the group. One hot, sunny day in the United Kingdom, I was working with a small coaching group. I offered the chance to work outside to enjoy the beautiful weather and to get some fresh air.

While most people relished the idea, there was one person who was against it. He was unhappy at the thought of leaving the boundary of our room. In the room, he felt safe and secure. He said that he would feel vulnerable working outside in the open air. Of course, we needed to honor this, so we remained in the breakout room.

Typical challenging situations prevented by focusing on the environment

Many petty challenging behaviors such as chatting, moaning, and complaining can relate to the group not liking their environment and feeling the need to express this in some way, either to you as the facilitator or to their colleagues.

If participants don't feel psychologically safe in their environment for whatever reason, it can show up in many forms. If a human being feels threatened, a fight/flight/freeze response will initiate. This response can manifest into many different behaviors, e.g., a flight response may show up as people folding their arms, remaining silent, not contributing, and even physically leaving the event. Focusing on creating psychological safety before, at the start, and throughout the event can suppress behaviors that surface from feeling threatened.

Your group may be worried about the event and what it involves. Upon arrival, if you and your room appear not to be ready to receive them, your attendees may start to worry about your ability to lead them through the event. Such concern may be expressed through initial hostility towards you, challenging questions being asked early on, or a general lack of engagement. How do you behave when you feel that you're not in safe hands?

Other challenging situations such as spillage from abandoned cups from a previous meeting or unpleasant smells from rubbish and discarded food not cleared away may also create an unsatisfactory environment leading to disruptions to your event.

CHAPTER 4

VENUE

Size matters, but so does location and layout

The previous chapter focused on how it felt in the room. This chapter will focus on the physical aspects of the venue. It will define an appropriate site is using three factors:

1. Location
2. Size
3. Layout

If the space allocated for the event isn't conducive to what it's trying to accomplish, dissent amongst the group will occur much more quickly. If your group is feeling deflated because of the venue they're in, you will have to work much harder to get them back into a positive frame of mind.

1. Location

For venue location, we will look at:

- The location of the room
- The impact of distance between the main room and breakouts
- The advantages of using an office or external venue
- Other vital considerations for selecting a location

The location of the room

Over the years, I have delivered events in many different places. Hotel conference rooms and corporate offices are the most common. In both hotels and offices, I've found myself running events in open spaces within the buildings rather than being assigned a room. I recommend avoiding this at all costs. The noise and distractions are too much.

In one hotel, I ran a Consulting Skills course in an atrium area, which was six stories high. Several glass-walled elevators continuously zipped up and down through the central core of the hotel, passing through the atrium on their way to other floors, which caused regular distractions and added to the noise level. The glass-walled elevators also caused safety and security problems. It's challenging to create emotional safety when members of the public are gawping at you through a glass-walled lift. It's also difficult to protect Intellectual Capital in such an environment. Worse still, it's difficult to hear what others are saying.

Everyone's voice had six floors of space to travel before bouncing off the ceiling. I obtained a few microphones and audio speakers so everyone could hear what people were saying. The microphones slowed down discussions immensely. I also brought in pinboards to try to create a sense of a room and provide valuable hanging space for flip charts, which could be angled away from public view. All this took extra time, effort, and money to sort.

In another example, when running a Customer Relationship Skills training event in an office, I was given the only conference room in the building, which was right next to the café. It was noisy with people regularly popping in for coffee as well as snacks and lunch. The event required the group to work at a deep experiential level to develop their relationship-building skills. The venue hindered such work because of the noise levels in the café. We ended up working outside a lot more than planned and conducting more activities in small groups where people could hear each other better.

Therefore, I recommend checking where in the building your room is located. Consider what implications there are for your event and group.

Where are the main room and breakout rooms located?

Make sure the distance between the main room and breakout rooms is as short as possible. The proximity of the rooms tends to be closer when using hotels because of coordinating refreshments. It can be trickier in the office because of the available space. In some events I've run, the breakouts have been on different floors and even in separate wings of a building. The high amount of travel time required for people to move from one room to another disrupted the schedule, reducing the amount of real work the group achieved.

If the distance is short, it reduces the travel time and limits the chances of participants wandering off (e.g., for a cigarette break or coffee). It also enables you to manage the agenda better with more time devoted to actual work.

In the office or an external venue?

There are benefits to running an event either in the office or using an external venue:

Benefits of using the office	Benefits of using an external venue
It's usually free of charge, with no risk of fees applied if the event is rescheduled.	The availability of space is unlimited. You can have a venue to fit your budget and needs exactly. The room is unlikely to be hijacked by other employees refusing to leave.
More familiar surroundings can make it easier for your group to adapt to and feel psychologically safe.	Participants won't get distracted by other employees in the building who are not invited to the event, especially those in the café.
It's easier to pop back to the desk to retrieve forgotten materials or resources.	Participants won't be easily found by their managers who want them to focus on other priorities.
It's more convenient for participants. They know where they're going and are less likely to get lost.	There's a dedicated service team to help you with the room setup, refreshments, and fixing audiovisual problems.
You know how everything works and where everything is.	The venue can feel special to the participants.
Easier access to leaders and experts in the building if help is needed.	It's easier for participants to focus on the event when away from the office.

Whichever you choose, make sure the venue works for you and your group.

Other considerations on venue location

Access to natural light – Natural light can have a significant impact on the behavior and mood of participants. Full-spectrum lighting (like natural light) works best to improve mood. It can create less anxiety and stress and improve overall health.[15] Conversely, a lack of natural light can invite fatigue amongst participants, especially if the lighting is poor. If the venue doesn't have natural light, I recommend adjusting the agenda and planning for more regular breaks so your group can get out into natural light.

Air quality – According to a North American study by Future Workplace entitled "The Workplace Wellness Study,"[16] natural light and air quality have the most significant impact on workplace wellness. Air quality was the biggest wellness factor that employees cared about in the study. The research cites poor air quality as making some employees sleepy during the workday. Ideally, your venue should have either effective air conditioning or at least the ability to open some of the windows to create natural ventilation.

> **Natural light and air quality have the most significant impact on workplace wellness.**

Accessibility - Can the room be accessed by those in your group who have a disability? If you're using a venue for the first time, it's worth checking how easy it is for folks to get to the room.

The duration of your event will determine how much the location impacts it. The longer it is, the more impact it will have. Participants will put up with an inferior place if it's only for an hour or two. If the event is more than half a day, then try to get a better location. If you can't switch locations, enhancing the feeling of the room can help as covered in the previous chapter. Putting up colorful posters, having brightly-colored sticky notes and markers on the tables, and playing welcoming music can uplift a drab and dreary space.

2. Size of venue

Very often, the size of the venue can be like living in the story of "Goldilocks and the Three Bears." Many of them are either too small or too big. Rarely are they precisely the right size. The important thing is to have enough space to meet the purpose of the event. We will look at what you can do when a room is too small or too big, assuming you're unable to change rooms.

> ***TOP TIP***
>
> *When checking the capacity of a venue, ask what layout relates to that number. Very often, the Salesperson will quote a capacity number based on a theater-style plan. If you want a cabaret-style design with round tables and chairs, that room's capacity will drop dramatically. Don't get caught out!*

When the room Is too small

If the room is too small, it will cause problems for you and your group. Generally. It can feel claustrophobic, and the room can heat up quickly. With too many people sharing the same space, the air can become stale. Poor air quality can make everyone feel very uncomfortable and sluggish. Even if you're lucky enough to have air conditioning, it may struggle to cope with too many people. The group will start to notice their discomfort rather than focusing on the event. As the pain grows, so will the dissent and challenging behavior. In this situation, you can give more breaks and use the breakouts more often. If the weather is warm, and with the group's permission, I sometimes take the group outside to run an activity.

If the room is too small, look to see if it's possible to take furniture out. If I'm running an event at an external venue, there are usually various tables available. Wherever possible, I ask for smaller tables, and in worst-case scenarios, I remove them altogether. Be mindful where you move the excess furniture. You need to make sure you're not creating a safety or fire evacuation hazard.

TOP TIP

If the room is too small, you will need to create space for you and your group to move around. If you can't move around the room, your ability to monitor progress on activities and deal with challenging behavior will be extremely restricted. Creating a sense of space in the place will also make it feel more inviting.

Getting rid of tables will be a trade-off between having the space you need to move around to access all the group and giving them desk space to put their stuff on. Having the right amount of space to run your event is usually more critical than putting your coffee cup somewhere. Make the room work for the event you're running and the activities you have planned within it.

When the room is too big

Linking back to my atrium experience, I had lots of space. It was vast. The volume of space created lots of problems, the biggest one being the need to use microphones. Using microphones slows discussions down because of the constant need to pass the microphone around the room. Not everyone feels comfortable speaking into a microphone, which inhibits some people from contributing.

Without microphones, everyone may struggle to hear what others are saying and become frustrated. If participants can't listen to a discussion, they will soon disengage.

What can you do when the room is too big?

Firstly, you can use microphones. Even if you have a loud voice that can project, others may not, and you want to make the event as inclusive as possible. If everyone's speaking volume is too low, frustration will quickly build.

The second thing you can do is to shrink the room by moving the tables closer together. You can use flip charts or pinboards to define the boundary around the tables. Shrinking the room and bringing everyone closer together can often negate the need for microphones and encourages your group to be more social. If they are too far apart from each other, the team bonding can often take longer. Make sure you leave enough space to access everyone in case they need help, or you need to manage their behavior. You can use any spare space from the shrinkage for running activities.

The third thing you can do if the room is too big is to change how you run the event. Switch from running discussions where everyone sits down to one where people stand working in groups around the room. Everyone can move around the room when each group presents. The movement not only shifts perspective but generates energy for the group. Getting everyone up and moving to a different part of the room can also break up any minor challenging behaviors which may be surfacing.

Having a bigger room than needed is a more pleasant problem to have. It will still take some thinking and planning to make the event work effectively and prevent challenging behaviors from surfacing.

3. Layout

There are many different room layouts. The key is determining which one is right for your event. We will look at some of the more common arrangements, providing a brief description of each and outlining how each one can work for you. We will discuss the benefits and problems of each design and the implications for managing challenging behaviors.

Cabaret layout

A cabaret layout uses table islands with chairs around them, creating table teams within the group. Participants can often feel safe in the room more quickly using this layout because of their sense of belonging within their table team. Safety can increase if participants who already know each other sit at the same table.

While participants who know each other (and sit together) can help accelerate emotional safety, it can also stimulate challenging behavior. The feeling of security amongst their table team can reduce the fear of being in a larger group. Generally, security is a good thing as the group will feel safe enough to contribute. However, participants who know each other will often vocalize their dissatisfaction with their peers if they're not happy about the event or certain aspects of it.

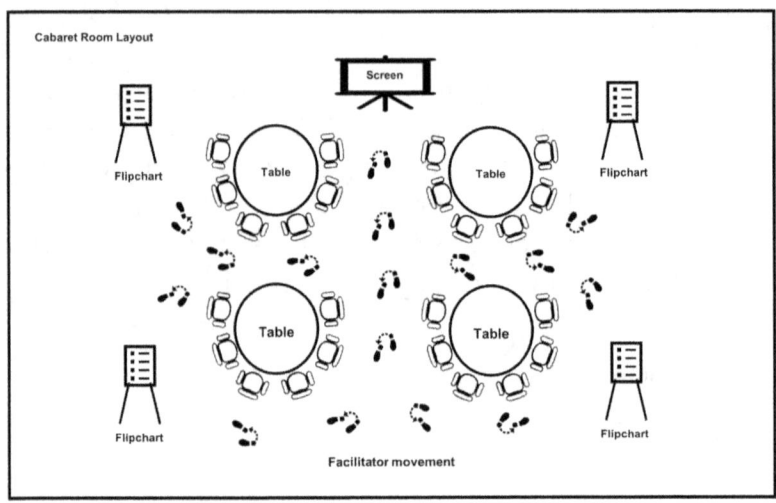

Benefits of Cabaret layout include:

- You can create table groups of similar or mixed experience/knowledge
- Participants often feel psychologically safer working in a smaller group
- Enhanced learning can occur when working in smaller groups
- The facilitator can easily access all table groups
- It's easier to move people to different tables and split pockets of challenging behavior
- You can create new table teams for specific activities

Problems of Cabaret layout include:

- It consumes a lot more space

- Challenging participants can often congregate together on a table

- It can be more expensive, requiring a bigger room to accommodate everyone

Cabaret is the most common layout used in training events because of the number of benefits it has. The ability to create new table teams during the event to suit different activities can help everyone learn from others. For example, if you have only a handful of experts in the room for a specific topic, you can spread them amongst the table groups to act as topic champions to help everyone else on the table. Alternatively, you can segregate them onto an expert table. If the experts can work on their own, more advanced challenging problems, it may prevent them from being frustrated by everyone else's slower pace.

U-Shaped Conference Layout

The U-Shaped conference layout is another favored layout for events because it allows everyone to see each other. It feels inclusive. It also enables you to come into the U and see what everyone is doing. Having excellent visibility is helpful for both monitoring progress and managing challenging behaviors.

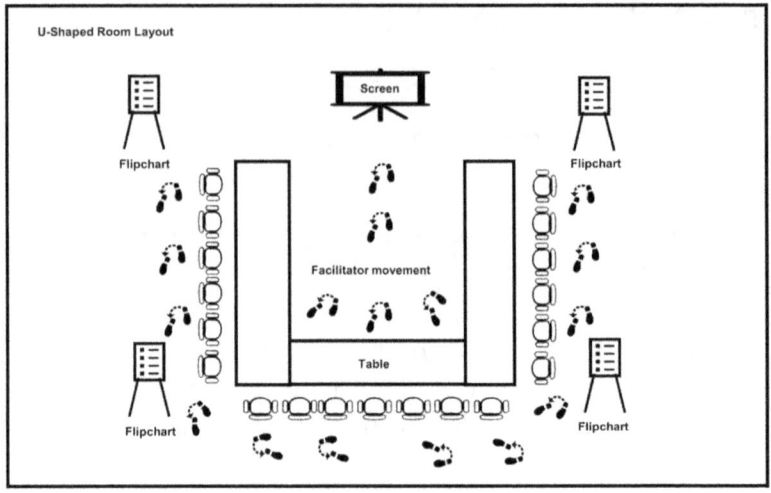

As in the cabaret layout, the ability to move participants around is simple. For example, get every second person to move two empty spaces clockwise. That way, they will sit next to two new people. Quick and easy!

While it doesn't lend itself for group work as well as the cabaret layout, you can create groups using this layout by utilizing the three sides of the U.

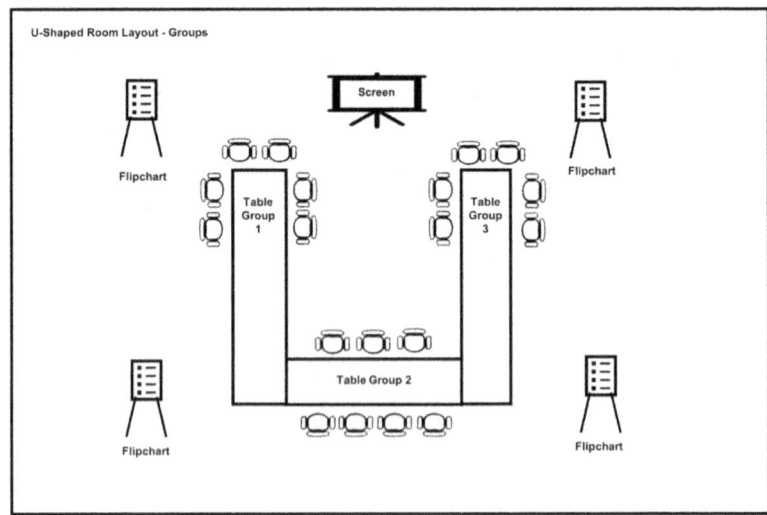

Benefits of U-Shaped Layout include:

- The facilitator can enter the U to connect better and manage all the participants and their progress
- Everyone is easily visible to the facilitator
- Creating sub-groups is still possible by using the three areas of the U
- Interaction is excellent as everyone talks into the U

Problems of the U-Shaped layout include:

- It may take more time for shy participants to speak up since it can feel more intimidating sitting in one large group
- It takes more time and effort to set up and form mini-groups for activities
- Participants at the end of each side of the U can often feel isolated

Generally, the U-shaped layout can effectively prevent challenging behaviors since everyone is visible not only to you but also to everyone else in the room. There's nowhere to hide.

Conference Room Layout

The conference room layout is typical when running events for organizations internally. Conference rooms tend to have a large, immovable table in them. The table and chairs tend to fit the room perfectly, reducing the ability to alter the layout. Cables are often threaded within the table, making it difficult to move. Power sockets on the table can tempt the group to get their devices out and charge them.

THE FEARLESS FACILITATOR

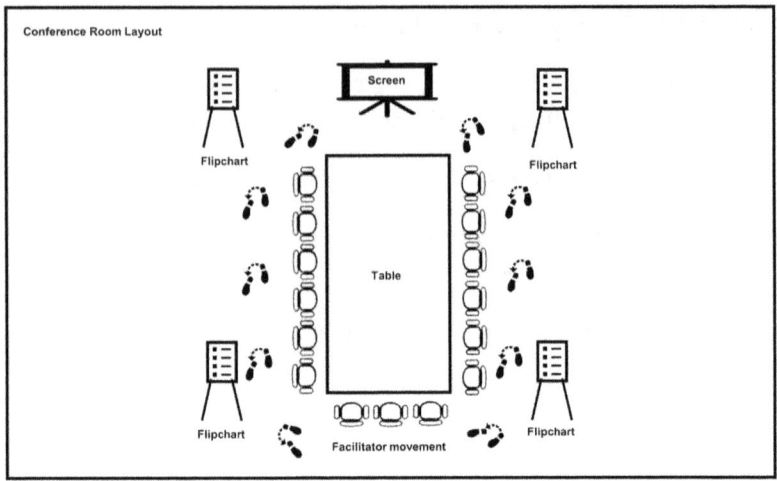

Benefits of Conference Room Layout

- There is plenty of desk space for materials and technology if needed

- There is usually lots of room for hanging flip charts on the walls

- The facilitator can sit at the table and feel part of the group rather than standing up. Operating at the same physical level can create more intimacy and parity among the group

- It can feel inclusive when everyone is sitting at the same table

Problems of Conference Room Layout

- Physical access to all the participants can be difficult, making any interventions for challenging behavior limited

- Sitting directly across a table from other participants can feel confrontational with an "us versus them" type atmosphere. The feeling will increase if certain factions of a team sit together and have strong, opposing views from others

- It's more challenging to work in groups because of the limited space around the table

- Some conference rooms have a second row of seats against the wall, away from the table. If some people are sitting in the so-called cheap seats, you may get a two-tier group. For example, those at the table may contribute more than those in the cheap seats

While the conference layout can work with smaller groups who need to come together as one team, it is harder to use this layout for high energy, free-flowing type events because of the large table in the middle of the room. Participants can still work in pairs or trios at the table. Alternatively, they can stand up and leverage the wall space to work on flip charts. The only challenge is everyone gathering around when each group presents back, but groups can take it, in turn, to present from the front.

TOP TIP

When there is limited space in the room, consider using a seating plan to mix up participants and break up any possible challenging behaviors expected from specific individuals.

U-Shaped chairs only layout

The U-Shaped chairs only arrangement can be used for dynamic events requiring lots of activity and movement amongst the group. You can either stand or sit at the front or be among the group. Your location in the U-shape can change depending on the desired impact. This layout works well when running discussions and for group work, where you have different activities require varying group numbers.

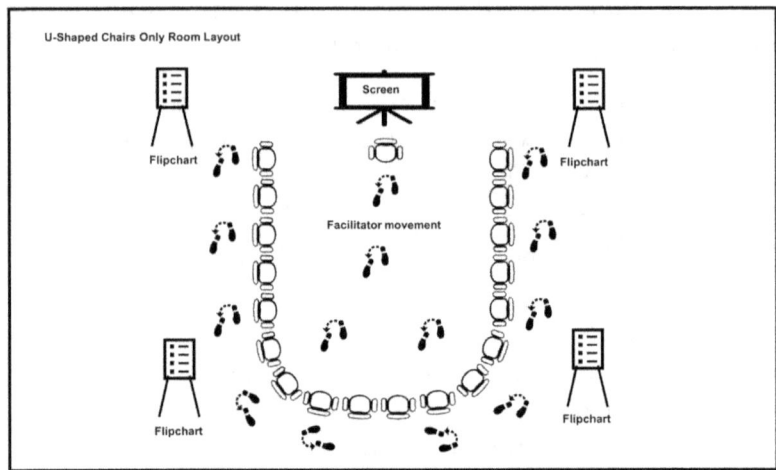

Benefits of the U-shaped chairs only layout

- U-shaped is quick to set up
- Easy for everyone to see each other
- It creates a sense of space in the room
- Dynamic in that you can create as many sub-groups as required since there are no tables
- The facilitator has plenty of options as to where to sit or stand
- Easy to get close to all the participants if there is a need to check progress or manage challenging behavior
- Encourages movement and networking, as there are no home tables

Problems of the U-shaped chairs only layout

- Participants can feel uncomfortable and even exposed without a table, providing a barrier between themselves and others in the room

- It can feel like group therapy for some participants

- There's nowhere to put materials and refreshments. Spillages can occur quite regularly, so be mindful of participants bringing in drinks without lids

- There is a capacity limit on participant numbers. The biggest group I've worked with on this layout is forty, and that required a big room to accommodate everyone. I needed a microphone to project my voice in the room

- Participants regularly misplace their belongings and materials because of all the movement around the room

The U-shaped chairs only layout can help if the event contains many activities requiring the participants to work in different group sizes. Participants can pair up, work in threes, fours, fives, etc. Due to the absence of tables, such groups can be set up and formed very quickly.

The absence of tables also prevents the formation of tribes within the group. When groups return from an activity, they will often try to sit back at their home tables. Without tables, there are no home tables, which encourages the participants to mix. Having chairs with wheels makes any movement quick and easy.

Which layout is best?

It depends. Choosing the best layout should be based on two main objectives:

1. Will the layout help achieve event success?
2. How effective will the layout be in managing the group and handling challenging behaviors?

There are many variables to consider when selecting the best layout, such as:

- Room availability
- Affordability
- The room capacity
- Ease of access
- Access to natural light
- Quality of ventilation

Challenging situations and behaviors can occur when the layout isn't suitable for the event you're trying to run and its objectives. For example, trying to run a free-flowing workshop using a theater-style layout with everyone sat in rows all facing forward won't work as well as the U-shaped chairs only layout. Group work and collaboration is limited in theater-style because the participants can't quickly move in their seat/row. Running a more formal event with U-shaped chairs only won't feel as appropriate compared to the Conference room layout. Participants expect structure (and tables) in a formal setting.

Typical challenging situations prevented by having an appropriate venue

The list of challenging conditions prevented by having a suitable venue is almost endless. People may be late due to traffic or not being able to find the site located in a strange building.

VENUE

They could be feeling irritated and flustered even before they've walked into the room. The agenda and timings are at risk if the distance between the main room and breakouts is too far away. Problems with fatigue due to poor air quality or lack of natural light may slow progress down and may prevent the group from achieving all the planned objectives. You will struggle to manage challenging behaviors if the layout is wrong, and you can't access all your group.

If the room is too big, you may incur unplanned costs by hiring microphones and audio speakers to help the group hear each other. Some spaces may look manageable in size, but the acoustics could make it hard to listen to people speaking. Running around the room with microphones during discussions will slow things down, impacting your plan, and limiting what you can achieve in the time available.

Challenging situations and behaviors can occur when the layout isn't suitable for the event.

If the room is too small, you may have to change your layout to fit. Access to your group may be limited. You may have to adjust your plan and turn planned activities into discussions due to the lack of room. Trying to work in groups when the room is too small can be a problem. Groups can struggle to work together because of the lack of space and surrounding noise from other groups, irritating them as the room hinders their progress.

Other challenging situations relating to the venue, which can cause irritation and frustration for you and your group can include the following:

- Problems with the audiovisual equipment (not working, can't connect to it, wrong cables, poor quality)
- Problems with low bandwidth wi-fi
- Poor quality refreshments

- Limited car parking facilities
- Limited toilet facilities
- Venue sign-in procedures and the need for visitor badges

TOP TIP

If you can, check the venue out before booking it. If not, at least ask for photos showing the layouts possible in it. Being there physically will enable you to feel how hot or cold the room is, what the noise levels are like surrounding the room, and how easy it is to find and get to the venue.

If the venue works for the group, they are free to focus on the event. If the venue doesn't work, participants will dwell on their discomfort and disconnect from the rest of the event.

CHAPTER 5

ENGAGEMENT

Building Relationships

Have you ever been to an event where you're the first (or one of the first) to arrive? It can feel quite awkward.

- Do you go up to the person who looks like they're in charge and say hello?
- Do you turn around, find coffee, and wait for others to arrive?
- Do you simply sit down and get your phone or laptop out while waiting for the event to start?

At my events, when the doors open, I am ready to receive the group. If I'm lucky, there's only a handful of people waiting initially. If so, I welcome each one into the room with a handshake and a smile. I learn the names of those first few people and try to keep them together to build common ground between them. As others arrive, I'm able to leave the initial group, who are by then chatting with each other. I repeat the process with others who enter the room.

If someone enters the room alone, I connect with them on a one-to-one basis and learn their name and something about them. I then introduce them to other people in the room to help them connect. For example, "Chris, let me introduce you to Sam and Alex. They're also keen golfers." Chris starts chatting with Sam and Alex, which allows me to walk away when the next person arrives.

Ideally, by the time the event is ready to start, the room looks, sounds, and feels like a cocktail party, but without the cocktails. Tea and coffee are great enablers to building engagement, as well. By helping the participants connect with each other straight away, the energy in the room at the beginning of the event is high and positive.

Contrast what I just described with an event where a facilitator rushes to complete final preparations while participants wander into the room to grab a seat. No one connects unless they already know each other. Some participants will get their phones or laptops out rather than talk to strangers in the room. Everyone is wondering who else in the room and where they fit in. The atmosphere can be quiet, reserved, and cautious. In my early years of being a facilitator, I failed to connect with the group before an event started. Consequently, it took a while for everyone to warm up and embrace the event.

Doing a meet and greet at the door and spending time to get to know people before the event begins takes energy and effort, and that requires physical resilience. However, building relationships early on is an investment in accelerating the group's engagement and psychological safety.

ENGAGEMENT

When people feel a sense of belonging, they feel safer. An increase in safety correlates with a willingness to contribute. People are more likely to speak up if they think it's safe to do so. A feeling of inclusivity can help create a positive experience at events. As discussed in Chapter 3, if participants feel positive and secure, they are less likely to display challenging behaviors. When there are fewer challenging behaviors to deal with, the overall event experience will be more positive, thus suppressing further challenging behaviors.

People are more likely to speak up if they think it's safe to do so.

This chapter is about how you can create engagement and maintain it, so the group has no desire to disrupt the event. To help increase engagement, we will look at three areas:

1. How to engage with participants
2. How to help the participants engage with each other
3. How to maintain engagement during an event

1. How to engage with participants

Work the Room

To engage with your group, you need to understand them and have the desire to help them. If you see the event as merely another hurdle, to get to the next payday, your group will sense it and will be less willing to engage, if at all. Your engagement will drive everyone else's.

As covered in the previous chapters, putting thought and effort into creating the right environment and securing an appropriate venue can indicate to your group you care about them. When they walk into a room, if participants feel valued because of how it looks and feels, they will be more likely to engage. It's then down to you to bring the event to life by engaging with them.

To do that, you will need to get to know the attendees. As well as asking a person their name and other trivial facts, some questions to consider asking include:

- What's your passion?
- What's your proudest moment so far this year?
- What are you hoping to get out of the event?
- What are your concerns about the event, if any?

When you first engage participants, they will often only talk about work and their role. Asking for trivial facts can feel transactional. You ask for specific information, and that's what they give you. Asking them about things like their passions and proudest moments gives them the freedom to disclose whatever they want at this early stage. It provides the respondent with the choice to talk about home or work. Getting participants to talk about their passions and interests can often ignite them. It connects them with the positive energy associated with their passion. The positivity can suppress any anxiety they may be having about attending the event.

Susan RoAne covers this topic extensively in her book *How to Work a Room.* Many of her tips on being successful at engaging with others are about making them feel comfortable, by being enthusiastic and energetic in the way you interact.[17]

Other questions asked at this early stage aim to understand why someone is attending an event. The objective is to gain insight into their expectations and concerns. You may not have time to cover all the questions with everyone you welcome into the room, so use whichever ones you feel comfortable asking.

It's important to remember that this must not feel like an interrogation where you quiz each person extensively. They're unlikely to want to share too much information unless you are prepared to do the same. Be intentional in what information you share, as that will set the tone for what the other person is willing to share.

How you connect

It's also essential to think about how you're engaging with your participants.

- Are you fully present with the person who's speaking?
- Are you paying full attention, giving good eye contact, and displaying positive body language, which affirms what the other person is saying?
- Are you noticing what the other person is saying, how they're saying it, and what they may not be saying?
- Are you merely soliciting facts or going deeper by seeing what emotions are displayed when they talk? For instance, if they sound excited or nervous about attending the event, noticing and validating them can help to empathize with that person and understand where they're at emotionally

You know you're actively engaging with the other person when the rest of the room goes out of focus. The other person will be able to tell if you're genuinely interested or going through the motions, so be careful.

2. How to help the participants engage with each other

As covered in Chapter 4, having an appropriate layout where the participants can engage with each other is a crucial success factor. Having an agenda where there are breaks for the group to connect can also help. Breaks should be long enough for people to chat with each other rather than merely having enough time for a bathroom break. Other opportunities could include having small group activities during the event, solving problems, listening to each other, and bonding through shared experiences.

Break the Ice

If the event agenda allows, starting with an icebreaker can accelerate group engagement. Even if some attendees know each other, they may know each other only at a superficial level. The purpose of the icebreaker is to knock down barriers among the group and create a positive, shared, high energy experience that will speed up group bonding. Such an experience will catapult the group into the rest of the event using the energy generated from the icebreaker. Creating shared experiences early on can also provide a talking point to discuss for the rest of the event. There are many icebreakers; the two that I often cover have multiple objectives:

- Get to know who's in the room
- Build common ground in the group
- Create energy early on by getting everyone active

Creating energy early on signifies to the group that they need to participate rather than remain passive. It sets the tone and manages expectations for the event. If your group is having a positive experience and getting value from it early on, their engagement will increase, and the chances of challenging behavior surfacing will decrease.

Building common ground in the group early on speeds up engagement by focusing on their similarities. When participants come together, their focus can be on their differences. Such an egocentric focus is especially true when participants from different teams come together.

Example 1—Finding Common Ground

The first icebreaker requires the group to get into trios (and fours if the numbers don't work out). Each trio gets ten minutes to find out about what they have in common with each other. They draw a Venn diagram, each circle representing one person in the trio.

During the ten minutes, the aim is to find at least one area of commonality at every point where the circles overlap. To make it more interesting, I encourage the group not to focus on work-related items, e.g., we all work for the same organization. Such examples are too easy and don't require any effort or thinking, limiting the value of the experience. Other ideas like, "we're all male" or "we're all from the United States," are equally lame and should be highlighted and discouraged before the start of the activity.

Having the people's names in each circle helps everyone else in the room connect the names to the areas of commonality for future reference. For example, if John and Sarah have a love of cooking and someone else in the room also shares that passion, they are more likely to seek out John and Sarah during a break to chat about it. Participants who share common interests now have a reason to engage in a conversation with each other.

Venn diagram—Finding common ground activity

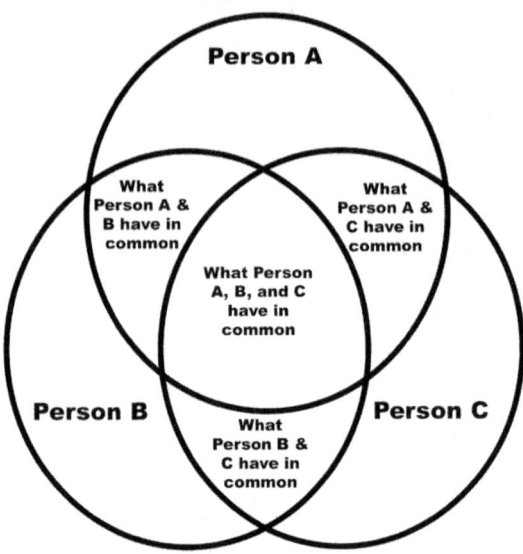

It's essential that you allow time for everyone to present to establish connections around the room. I'm always amazed at what people have in common. In one example, two people who hadn't met before the event were both planning a vacation to Peru to climb Machu Picchu. During a break, they talked about their respective trips and discovered not only would they be there at the same time, but they would most likely see each other during the climb. They went from not knowing one another to building a great relationship—during the event.

Example 2—Introductions

The other icebreaker can be done with the whole group or smaller groups. It involves asking the participants to introduce themselves to the rest of the group using a question or two, e.g., What's your favorite hobby? What's the one thing the rest of the group is unlikely to know about you?

Ask for a volunteer to go first and then ask someone else to follow on from the first person by building on what the first person said. For example, let's say a person talked about their passion for hiking or having kids (family is their passion). The rest of the group would listen, and then someone else who could connect to the previous person would go next. Perhaps the next person is a parent or also loves hiking.

This process would continue until everyone has introduced themselves. The realization that everyone can connect to someone else in the room with an interest or passion can be uplifting as each person realizes they have something in common with at least one other person in the room.

Common ground icebreakers can help lift engagement by reducing the feeling of isolation within a group.

Beware of creeping death

I've seen a lot of facilitators (and I used to be one of them) run "creeping death" type introductions where everyone introduces themselves, in turn, starting from one end of the room to the other. This process works well when the objective is simply to understand who's in the room quickly. However, if you ask people to do any more than that, it can become a problem.

Creeping death takes away the choice of when people speak to the rest of the group for the first time. Some participants will begin to panic and focus only on their introduction, so they don't mess it up and look foolish. Others will start analyzing the line to see how long they have before it's their turn to present. They don't listen. They are not engaged.

"Creeping Death" introductions are called that for a reason. They suck energy from the room. If you use them, keep them short and sharp, and move on.

TOP TIP

The level of apathy can rise quickly if some participants take too long to introduce themselves. Ensure you provide guidance on each person's allotted time and stick to that time as much as possible. I often go first to show the group what I want from them.

3. How to maintain engagement

Getting the attention of an audience when presenting is easy. Keeping it is the problem. It's the same when facilitating an event. Your group will usually consist of very busy people with lots of priorities and demands on their time. They will initially give you the benefit of the doubt even if they are skeptical about the event or have other concerns. However, participants will quickly decide whether the event is a worthwhile investment in their time. If the event isn't working for them, they will initially vote with their minds and disengage. If things don't improve, they may even vote with their feet and leave. Here are some of the more helpful ways to maintain engagement once you've established it.

Keep it real

The critical question that any participant will ask is, "What's in it for me?" Participants want to know what they will get out of the event and how it will help them. Ideally, the event purpose and goal (see Chapter 1) will match the needs of the group (see Chapter 6). Validating the event purpose with the group can help manage their expectations.

A group will initially engage if the event sounds relevant to them. Relevance is the answer to the question, "What's in it for me?" However, while the topics (what the event will cover) seem relevant, how they are covered can enhance or detract from the relevance.

For example, as I write this, I'm on my way to run a leadership event that aims to help new leaders improve how they give feedback to their direct reports. For the skills practice part of the workshop, I could have used roleplay scenarios from another, similar event. Instead, I asked those attending the event what typical situations they find difficult. Using this data, I have created some roleplays that will resonate with the group. The group is more likely to engage because they know they will benefit from the learning and be able to apply it the next time they are facing that scenario.

While some participants may be happy having the opportunity to practice whatever the scenario is, some will appreciate the value in practicing situations they've experienced and struggled with in the past.

Wherever possible, working on problems related to the group's real world will increase relevance and engagement. It will require extra work to understand what the group's real world is, but the work will pay off through the increased engagement, learning, and real-world benefits gained.

My aim for this event is to enable the group to feel more confident and competent in giving their team members better feedback.

Current Issues

Another way to increase relevance is to work on current issues. Roleplay requires participants to pretend to be someone else while practicing a skill. Real play requires participants to be themselves rather than reading from a script. Practicing skills such as listening, and coaching are examples of where real play can work well. In a coaching example, one person can practice their coaching skills, and the other can work on a real issue.

Both people get value from the activity as one person gets to practice the skill, and the other gets to work on their problem.

Working on current issues can often deepen the relationships among the group members as they learn more about each other and their challenges. When participants help each other succeed, their bond strengthens.

TOP TIP

Whatever activity you use to practice skills, there needs to be an effective debrief. The group will benefit from having time to reflect on how they can transfer their learning to their real-world context.

Balancing the experience

Our ever-reducing attention spans mean that participants will very quickly switch off if they don't like their experience. There needs to be variety in an event rather than simply doing more of the same. The mixture can include learning discussions, activities, reflection time, and small group work. Running events where the group is in receive mode—listening to subject matter experts all day, and not doing anything—will be incredibly hard work for them. Their short-term memories will be full before lunch, rendering the afternoon presentations redundant.

Similarly, doing lots of activities all day with no time for reflection and learning will be exhausting and offer limited insight. Variety can help keep the group engaged.

Unless you know your group very well, it's hard to predict what they will prefer to do at an event. Some participants love roleplays, while others love standing up and presenting in front of a group. Some attendees love discussing theory. The best way to engage everyone is to offer a variety of ways for them to participate.

Take a moment to reflect on what you enjoy during an event and think about how that preference influences how you shape your events.

Celebrate Success

Momentum at an event is incredibly helpful in getting things done. If participants are engaged, enthusiastic, and energized, anything is possible. When the group achieves something, celebrate success in some way. Examples of achievement can include things like:

- Reaching a decision
- Completing an activity
- Solving a problem
- Resolving a conflict

How to celebrate will often vary depending on culture and the group itself. Taking time to celebrate achievements can be rewarding. It can create the impetus to do more to feel the same elation again.

Conversely, providing no recognition can be demotivating and demoralizing for the group. They may feel they merely have to survive and get to the end. There's little engagement other than to get done what's needed and be released from the event.

> **The celebration needs to be relevant and valued by the group for it to mean something.**

Celebrating success is also about gratitude. Being grateful and appreciative of efforts made by the group is essential to encourage continued engagement. For those who were reluctant, worried, or skeptical about the event, receiving recognition from everyone on their effort and achievement so far can be motivational if done authentically.

> **TOP TIP**
>
> *If you can take time to understand what celebrating success means for the group, using that throughout the event can help keep attendees engaged. Celebrations could mean a coffee break, an early finish, recognition on social media, ice creams or treats, drinks after the event, or something else. The celebration needs to be relevant and valued by the group for it to mean something.*

Move and mix them

Have you ever been to an event where you're in a small group, and there are one or two people in that group you find challenging? They're always talking, ignoring your (and others') ideas, trying to be in charge all the time, or generally trying to bully others. Perhaps you've found yourself in a group where no one wants to take charge and make decisions, and they all look to you to lead. It gets worse when you realize you will remain in that group for the rest of the event.

Some groups work well at an event, and others do not. Leaving them like that can split the group into two, with one half having a great time and engaged, while the other half are looking to kill each other or leave the event (fight/flight modes).

The danger of moving people around and mixing them up is that you break up the cohesion of groups that are working well. The consequence of doing nothing may result in the disgruntled half of the group descending into mutiny. The mutineers may start creating significant problems in the broader group, which affects everyone's overall experience.

If people know they will get to move from group to group regularly, it not only increases the variety as they will be working with different people, but it also signals to them that if they get a challenging group, it won't be for long.

For some events, this may not be possible due to specific teams needing to work together on a joint problem. Such teams can still mix by working in pairs or trios.

If you can find ways of mixing up people, not only will this create energy in the physical movement, but it will also create a new dynamic within each new group, bringing new learning. Participants will learn how to work with different people quickly and effectively. They will also learn how to handle different personalities to collaborate and build consensus. If participants feel they are learning and not stuck in a particular group, they will engage. Guidance on how to move people can be found in Chapter 15.

Typical challenging situations prevented by focusing on engagement

The obvious one here is preventing disengaged participants. A lack of engagement may show up in many ways ranging from participants looking at their phones to someone walking out. If some people are not focusing on the event, they're most likely doing something else. That's tough to manage. A lack of engagement can erode the possibility of the event achieving its objectives or at least some of the participants not getting any value from it. If there's no engagement, there's no learning, no buy-in, and no real progress.

A benefit of bringing people together is to build relationships. If they are working together to solve a problem, decide, or debate an issue, the bond between them strengthens. If people are not engaged, the capacity to build relationships will reduce, impacting collaboration and cooperation. A feeling of isolation among the group could occur without the support of others preventing people from feeling psychologically safe in the room. If fear and suspicion dominate the room, this will feed the desire to hold back, continuing the reluctance to engage.

CHAPTER 6

NEEDS

Understand needs, manage expectations

I once ran a training event on how to run workshops for a client team. The team would be running internal workshops across its organization as part of a broader transformation initiative. I spoke to the Sponsor (Bob) before the event to understand the context. I wanted to include content that was helpful to the team. I asked Bob if he would open the event to explain its objectives and my role. He agreed.

Bob opened the event but said only a few words. I don't remember his exact words, but they went something like this.

"Welcome, everyone. Thanks for coming. Paul's come along to teach you how to run great workshops. I'm sure you're going to have a great day. I'll be back later to see how it's going. Paul, over to you."

With that, Bob left the room. I assumed everyone knew about the context given Bob's short introduction.

I explained the plan and objectives for the group. I immediately saw a lot of puzzled faces staring back at me. My key facilitator mantra is, "If in doubt, check it out," so I did. I shared with the group that, to me, they looked puzzled. I asked them if they knew why they were here. No one had a clue. No one knew about the role of running workshops in the transformation. Everything had to stop! While I had some insights, it was not appropriate for me to share them as an external facilitator.

Someone volunteered to find Bob and bring him back. When he came back, the group got very hostile very quickly. They were annoyed with their new role and lack of consultation. They were even more annoyed that I seemed to know more than they did. Bob had miscalculated the reaction of the group, and he was now paying the price. I offered to facilitate a discussion to mediate a way through the situation. Bob declined and asked me to step out of the room while he dealt with it.

An hour later, the door opened, and the group spilled out of the room. Bob informed me that the event would not go ahead. Some of the group felt very strongly about the situation. One person threatened to get the local workers union involved, while others wanted help from human resources. It took another month for me to return and complete the workshop. Even then, the group was not as excited and committed as other groups I've had the pleasure of facilitating.

The above story is about meeting needs. Bob didn't brief his team about the transformation and their new role. His team needed transparency and dialogue on the role change before the event. Bob needed a commitment from his team, which he didn't get, and the event failed as a result.

The team had other needs; namely, they needed to understand why they were attending the event. The benefits were also unclear. Employees may be willing to accept change if they know what's in it for them.

I messed up too. I failed to specify my needs for Bob to open the event in a way that would help his team. We agreed that Bob would do the introduction. I didn't spend enough time explaining the need for him to cover the context of the event and its objectives. As a result, I got an immediate push back when I tried to progress with the workshop.

Challenging situations and behaviors can occur when participants feel that an event is not what they expected or doesn't meet their needs. This chapter will look at understanding and meeting the needs of your group in three steps:

1. Understanding context to meet needs
2. Priming stakeholders
3. Setting pre-work

1. Understanding context to meet needs

Understanding the event context can help uncover your group's needs. Once clarity on the context is known, you can design your event to reflect the context to meet the group's needs. No one likes unpleasant surprises. If any needs can't be met, use priming to manage the group's expectations as soon as possible.

Delaying the briefing to a group until the event may hinder initial progress with participants clarifying what the event is about and how it affects them. As in the opening story in this chapter, the event may even have to stop altogether.

Understanding the context first will inform how you prime folks later. There are four critical aspects of context to consider.

a) What else is going on in the organization?

b) Have there been previous events?

c) Is there any challenging history among the group?

d) Are there any sensitive topics?

a) What else is going on in the Organization?

Understanding what else is happening within the organization can help address the group's need for reassurance. For instance, receiving an invitation to an event when the organization has recently announced job losses may alarm some people. The invite may imply they are affected somehow. Knowing what else is going on can help shape the design, content, and tone of an event. Other things that might be going on could include:

- Restructuring
- Organizational takeover or merger
- A new boss
- Change in working practices
- Change in employee terms and conditions
- Change in the budget, pay, bonuses, pensions

Before the event. During event planning, ask the Sponsor how the event relates to what else is going on. If there's a direct link, the Sponsor should brief the group and provide them with an opportunity to ask questions before the event. The group may need time to come to terms with the news before being ready to engage positively. Even if there's no link, the Sponsor should say so to provide reassurance.

At the event. Get the Sponsor to open the event to remind the group of the situation. You will need to be sensitive to the feelings of the group, depending on the context. Using a more empathetic tone and approach may be appropriate. You will need to demonstrate that you're fully aware of their situation.

b) Have there been previous events?

Understanding what's happened beforehand can help address a group's need to continue to make progress. If past sessions didn't go so well, what needs to happen differently next time to avoid repeating the same mistakes? If it did go well, understanding what contributed to that could help create a similar experience.

The latest event may need to build on a previous one. Knowing what was covered and achieved before can help avoid covering the same ground or missing a vital step. Repetition can lead to frustration amongst the group. Skipping a crucial step could create confusion. Reminding the group what happened previously can help to hit the ground running at the latest event.

Before the event. Find out from the Sponsor and the group what happened previously. Get both perspectives, if possible. They may be different. Knowing what worked and what didn't the last time will help shape the design of the latest event. Building on what was covered and achieved already will help the group continue making progress.

At the event. Briefing the attendees on how the current event relates to previous ones can be done before or during the event. The group should be aware of any required changes in their behavior and what's expected of them at the current event to succeed.

c) Do the participants attending have challenging history between them?

Understanding the team dynamics and personalities within the group can help address the group's need for harmony during an event. Is there tension or conflict between individuals or teams which requires proactive mitigation? For example, don't sit them next to each other or across from each other.

Before the event. Find out from the Sponsor if there are likely to be any personality clashes or other possible challenging group dynamics. They may have recommendations on how to deal with such issues. Talking to the participants can also reveal hints of where group dynamic problems may surface. Use your findings to adjust your event design where possible. Items to think about include:

- Which room layout will work best to support group dynamics?
- Is there a need for a seating plan to split people up?
- Should the group work in specific groups or one big group?
- Will building in time for a common ground icebreaker help?

At the event. As well as ensuring you set up a social contract to reinforce expectations on behavior, it would be helpful for the Sponsor to make everyone aware of the benefits of their cooperation. You may also need the Sponsor to be present throughout the event to help manage group dynamics.

d) Are there sensitive topics the group will find irritating if mentioned?

There is always a need for sensitivity with a group. The challenge is finding out what topics could potentially derail the event.

I've experienced potential derailment many times during learning discussions when one person goes off on a tangent, which gets everyone agitated. For example, we could be talking about how to improve employee engagement. Suddenly, someone starts venting about a lack of pay raises or bonuses. Before too long, the whole group starts moaning, and the topic of improving employee engagement is lost. Even worse, such a derailment can create negative energy, which can be hard to shift and can linger for the rest of the event.

Before the event. Find out from the Sponsor what topics the group may find sensitive. There could be sensitivities linked to recent announcements on pay, bonuses, promotions, or changes in working practices. Understanding what else is going on in the organization will give you a sense of potentially sensitive topics.

At the event. If it's a time of high sensitivity for everyone, the Sponsor may need to be present throughout to show solidarity and support. If the group does erupt and deviate, they need to be aware of the consequences, e.g., reduced breaks, later finish time, or a priority item dropped from the schedule. Providing the group with a choice of what to do next can help diffuse a situation, e.g., let the group vent or park it and move on.

2. Priming Stakeholders

Once you have spoken to the Sponsor and the group about their needs, you can begin to prime them. Priming simply means preparing stakeholders for an event. It's about telling them what they need to *know* and *do* before the event. You may need time between researching the context and priming everyone, depending on how much effort is required to translate their needs into a design for the event. The design will reflect the needs of the group and Sponsor as well as identifying your needs.

The stakeholders must be clear about what you need from them to make the event successful. Researching the context helps to understand your stakeholder needs, whereas priming helps to communicate your needs.

Priming your participants

It can be nerve-wracking for participants joining an event and being unsure of what to expect. The uncertainty can manifest into many different challenging behaviors. Reactions can range from a reluctance to join in (flight) to aggressive behavior (fight) where someone is continually pushing for answers on why they're there and what's in it for them.

Providing clarity before the event can help allay participant fears and concerns. Once they understand what to expect and the benefits of attending, participants tend to have a more open, positive frame of mind. Other benefits gained from talking to your group before an event include:

- Prime them on the need to complete any pre-work

- Briefing them on the content to be covered can help accelerate their thinking. Being prepared allows participants to hit the ground running at the event

- Getting to know each person and their interests can help build the relationship

- Providing an opportunity for each participant to ask questions to address their fears and concerns about the event
- You can inform your stakeholders which needs (captured in the context stage) will not be discussed at the event to help manage participants' expectations

When your group arrives at the event, they should already feel part of it because of the pre-event chat. They know what they're walking into and what they are likely to get out of it. No unpleasant surprises!

Priming the Sponsor

What do you want the Sponsor to say and do at the event? Understanding the context will provide clarity on what messages and actions the Sponsor should execute. Discussing the actions in advance will help them prepare.

Very often, the Sponsor can quickly delegate responsibility for the event to the facilitator, but they can play a vital role in its success. For example, when researching context, if the participants are unhappy about the planned topics, the Sponsor may need to play a supportive role in the event. Event success could be at risk without Sponsor support.

If the Sponsor needs to open the event, check what they're going to say. The messaging will affect how the group embraces the event. There may be value in coaching the Sponsor on how to communicate their message to the group.

> *TOP TIP*
>
> *If you want a sponsor to share key messages to the group, be as specific as possible. Then, get the Sponsor to playback what they heard. A few times, I have discussed with a sponsor what needs to be said. They've nodded in*

agreement only to then talk about something completely different at the event. It's as though something got lost in translation. Getting the Sponsor to play back what they are going to say ensures the messages are consistent with the intention and desired outcomes of the event.

Having the Sponsor at your event can add credibility to it. Trying to drive a session without any apparent sponsorship can create challenging situations. Participants often challenge why they should take an event seriously if their Leaders don't appear to be. The lack of leader presence reduces the credibility of an event or topic in the group's eyes.

Over the years, I have learned that it's essential to be explicit about what you need the Sponsor (and other leaders) to *say* and *do*. Very often, leaders will open an event and leave. If you need them to be present throughout, say so.

Who else do you need to Prime?

If you're running an event for a Sponsor, they need to be aware of what you need to make it a success. Examples will include:

- Size of venue
- Room layout
- Number of breakout rooms (size and layout)
- Audiovisual needs
- Catering needs
- Lighting
- Accessibility

You may have other needs. It's important to share your needs with whoever is responsible for the event booking to ensure you have the best chance of success.

3. The need for pre-work

If participants are primed, they should feel confident that the event will meet their needs, and that there's value attending an event. Your group can then progress to the next level of commitment. The next level of commitment is doing some work before the event. There is value in setting pre-work for an event. However, it needs to be relevant to the event.

> *TOP TIP*
>
> *Don't set pre-work which won't be used during the event or isn't relevant. Participants who have spent time and effort completing the work will quickly become annoyed when they realize they have wasted their time and effort. They will begin to wonder how else you may waste their time.*

Benefits of setting pre-work include:

- It sets the tone of active participation for the event itself

- It will accelerate the participants' thinking for the event and associated topics. The work may lead to more helpful, in-depth discussions at the event based on the work already done and knowledge gained

- It will start to build common ground as the participants will arrive at the event with at least one thing in common—their pre-work experience

- It reduces the chances of participants being surprised at the start of an event. If participants have done their pre-work, they have a better idea of what to expect

- When participants do the groundwork beforehand, you can optimize the time at the event. For instance, if an important decision needs to be made, the pre-work could be to gather all the data required to make an informed decision. If not, valuable time could be lost looking for data and documents during the event

- Pre-work can help get everyone up to the same level of understanding on a topic. Those who know less may have to do more work before the event. The benefit is enabling everyone to contribute equally to the event. It can reduce the gap between the experts and the less-informed, thus avoiding a "them versus us" split in the room

Any pre-work instructions given to the group need to be foolproof. Specifically, instructions must be as clear and concise as possible. They should cover three key elements:

- Output – What needs to be done?

- Process – What process to follow?

- Time – When does the output need to be completed?

Ideally, the pre-work should be sent well ahead of time (between one and two weeks before the event), to give everyone enough time to complete the work. Also, consider making the pre-work as engaging as possible. Giving out interesting pre-work can encourage the participants to engage early with the event. If the pre-work is dull, the participants will not only expect the event to be the same, but it may also reduce their willingness to do the pre-work.

TOP TIP

Check-in with the participants after the pre-work instructions are issued. Check that the instructions make sense, and they are progressing with the work. If not, some participants won't do it and will use every excuse under the sun to explain away their lack of action, including "my dog ate my pre-work." A short, personal message can have a significant impact on participants.

Challenging situations prevented by managing stakeholder needs

Sponsors can derail an event even before it's started. Their absence, communicating unhelpful messages at the kick-off, walking out, not sharing vital information beforehand, and failing to provide reassurance to their teams are only some derailment examples. All these can lead to participants being suspicious, cautious, and reluctant to engage at an event. The group may start to question the value of the event or decide to disengage very early on, making it difficult to recover the situation.

If the participants feel that an event doesn't meet their needs, they may not even turn up. If they do, they may behave like hostages forced to be in the room because they don't see the value.

Even if the topics sound relevant, if the group fails to connect what's happening at the event to their world, they will struggle to see the relevance and benefits. People are busy and need to optimize their time, so sitting in what seems to be a pointless meeting can quickly irritate and frustrate them. While politeness may ensue in the short-term, the group's behavior will soon deteriorate if things don't improve.

Ultimately, if you can understand and manage the needs of the stakeholders, you're more likely to be able to manage their behavior.

CHAPTER 7

TEAM

Many hands make light work

Wherever possible, I try to run events with more than one facilitator. Many hands make light work. One story that best illustrates the benefits of using a facilitator team is the time I ran a train-the-trainer event for a new group.

The team desperately needed the training to grow their trainer pool and train their technical recruits, but they had only a small budget to run the event. A local university offered one of their lecture rooms for free. The team would be potentially looking to recruit some of its graduates, so the university was keen to help. It was summer recess for the university, so they didn't need their lecture rooms.

Although I knew the course very well, I also knew it could be extremely demanding, both physically and mentally.

I wanted to share the load with a member of my team. It created a solution where everyone benefitted. I got extra help, my co-trainer would gain valuable experience in delivering the course, and the group would get support from another facilitator.

As part of our planning before the event, we discussed which modules each of us would own. As the lead trainer and owner of the course, I could deliver any of the modules, so I invited my co-trainer to pick which ones he preferred based on his prior experience. The preparations were going well. We both lived locally to the venue, so we traveled together the day before the event to set up. Thank goodness we did!

Although the room was big enough (barely), it was so full of tables and chairs you could not move around. There were enough tables and chairs to accommodate well over thirty-five students, and we were expecting around twenty participants.

We both felt incredibly frustrated. We knew that it would take time and effort to rearrange the room, so our preparation would take much longer than anticipated. It was a hot, sunny day, and it would be sweaty work. Before rolling up our sleeves, we discussed our options, both of us producing some good ideas on how to make the room work.

There was no one around to help. The hallway outside the room was narrow, so there was no way to move the excess furniture out there. We did have a small storage area adjacent to our room, and that was big enough to store all the excess chairs. As for the large, heavy tables, we sacrificed the front of the room and stacked them there. We created two tiers. The second tier of tables had their tops facing inwards to create additional flip chart hanging space.

After an hour of lifting and shifting, the room looked much better. There was enough space for everyone to sit comfortably and for us to move amongst the group. The room was no longer a dark, overfilled lecture room; it was now a light and airy workspace.

I could not have done all that work on my own in the time available. My co-facilitator and I both produced ideas that we implemented. We shared the burden of lifting and shifting. The joint effort enabled the room to be ready in half the time it would have taken one person.

This chapter will focus on the benefits of facilitating events with a team (or at least one other facilitator). It will cover the benefits to you and your group. This chapter will also reveal what sort of challenging situations you can avoid by deploying a facilitator team.

Benefits to you as the facilitator

I deliberately start with benefits to you rather than starting with your group. If you don't look after yourself first, it's challenging to be able to look after your group. Also, the benefits to you as a facilitator can have a positive effect on the group. If you're supported physically and mentally, you will be more able to help your group. There are three main benefits:

1. You get a break
2. You can give and get feedback
3. You get support to manage the event

Benefit 1. You get a break

When you're running an event alone, your group members will often come up to you during a break to ask a question. You don't get much of a break. When you have support, you can have a break when others are facilitating.

I have run events in a facilitator team and alone. While it's possible to run events on your own, the longer they are, the harder it will be, and the higher the toll on you both physically and mentally. As your energy drops, your enthusiasm and passion could begin to drop too. Your reduced engagement may negatively impact the event and the group.

Reasons why having a break is important

- By having a break, you can re-energize your mind and body and be ready for your next segment. If your last section didn't go well or a challenging situation occurred, the break will give you time to calm down (if required). You can shake off any lingering negative emotions and regroup before taking on the next segment

- A break will give you the breathing space needed to reflect on how you've been performing and get feedback from your co-facilitator. You can then adjust your approach as required to meet the needs of the group better. For example, you may have answered too many questions rather than facilitating the group to answer them. Having an opportunity to reflect on this and adjust your approach will help to avoid repeating the same mistake

Ultimately, having a break and letting someone else facilitate for a while will improve your chances of performing at your best when needed. It's tough to be at your best all day. The group will also benefit from you having a break, as they will get the best from both you and the other facilitator.

TOP TIP

If you're not in a facilitator team and flying solo, ensure the schedule contains plenty of breaks, so you and the group get time and space to recover from the work. Ideally, each segment should be no longer than ninety minutes. Concentration levels will drop massively beyond this.

Benefit 2. You can give and get feedback

Working as a facilitator team provides an excellent opportunity to provide constructive feedback on how the other facilitator is performing. Usually, there would be a mixture of things that went well and some things that could have gone better. Understanding what made a module go well using observed examples can help connect your actions with outcomes. Your co-facilitator may notice events differently to you, offering a fresh perspective.

Reasons why having feedback is important

- Providing feedback during the event will enable any required changes to be made when most needed. Waiting until the event has ended to discover what you could have done to make it better from the group is like shutting the door after the horse has bolted; it's too late

- Understanding what's working well during an event can help to enhance the event experience further. The group will benefit from any adjustments made since they will have a better experience

TOP TIP

Before the event, meet with your team to agree on the facilitator contract (how you want to work together). The contract can include what areas to give feedback on and when to provide feedback.

If you want feedback on your performance, you will need your team to pay attention during your segment. Without explicitly requesting this, the team may be planning on doing other things during your part, such as preparing for their session, checking their emails, or stepping out to have an extended break. Be clear on what you need from them and how you can meet the needs of your team.

Benefit 3. Being supported

There are many ways a co-facilitator can help you during an event. Here are some of the more common forms:

- Handling participants who are displaying challenging behavior while you continue to drive from the front
- Running errands such as checking if the refreshments/lunch is available or following up on missing printing or stationery
- Signaling when time is running out
- Offering advice when making a difficult decision
- Helps to move furniture during the setup
- Acting as a scribe and capture participant input on a flip

Reasons why being supported is important

- You can focus on the group and helping them make progress while your team deals with everything else
- Trying to multi-task can slow everything down. Progress may take longer if you're trying to manage too much
- The group's overall experience will feel much smoother as your team takes care of everything behind the scenes

Explain to your team what support you're likely to need and find out how you can help them. For instance, if you know you are weak at managing the time, asking your co-facilitator to give you time prompts from the back of the room can help you stay on track.

Another example is using your co-facilitator as a sounding board when making a difficult decision; they may have a different perspective on a situation from the back of the room compared to you at the front. Comparing the two views may influence and change your decision on how to deal with a situation.

Benefits to the group

There are many benefits to the group from having more than one facilitator. If there's only one facilitator and the group doesn't click with that person, there's no other option available. The group won't get a break from the facilitator they don't get on with, and their event experience could be disappointing. There are three main benefits to the group by having more than one facilitator:

1. Variety
2. The best person for each segment
3. If one facilitator drops out, the show can go on

Benefit 1. Variety

If there are two facilitators, the group will get more variety at the event. If the facilitators have different styles, the participants will receive a more rounded experience.

TEAM

Differences in facilitation style could include:

High energy	⇆	Low energy
Task-oriented	⇆	People-oriented
Excellent time management	⇆	Poor time management
Serious approach	⇆	Light-hearted approach
Detail-oriented	⇆	Strategy/big picture-oriented
Prefers theory and discussion	⇆	Prefers activities

A change is as good as a rest. Changing facilitators can give the group an energy boost. The shift required to focus on someone different can be enough to boost energy and concentration, leading to increased participation.

Changing facilitators can give the group an energy boost.

Each facilitator will have their preferred style. Embrace this. It shouldn't matter how you reach the objectives, so long as you reach them. If a facilitator tries to imitate someone else's style, their authenticity will erode as will their performance and impact. Participants appreciate authenticity, and it's much easier to focus on the needs of the group when you're not trying to be someone else.

Benefit 2. The best person for the job

Ideally, before the event, the lead facilitator will spend time with the team allocating segments to each member. The lead facilitator should be able to cover any of the sections. The rest of the group, who may be less experienced or knowledgeable, can choose which segments they would prefer to run. The allocation is typically done based on the experience, skill level, subject matter knowledge, and confidence levels concerning each part.

The allocation aims to ensure that the group gets the best person for the job each time.

> *TOP TIP*
>
> *If you have a facilitator team, there must always be a Lead Facilitator to make the difficult decisions where required. While the co-facilitator can provide input, there needs to be a recognized authority to make the call where necessary. Agree on who the overall leader is before the start of the event.*

Benefit 3. The show must go on

If you're delivering an event on your own and become sick, or there's an emergency at home, the event will have to be canceled and rescheduled. For example, on one occasion, during a two-day event, I slowly lost my voice on the afternoon of day one. It became so bad that my co-facilitator (Keith Burgess) had to step in and run the activity debriefs.

By the end of day one, I could hardly speak. Keith closed the day on my behalf. I recovered a little on day two, but again, Keith did more than planned to save my voice for the essential content I needed to cover.

At a different event, my co-facilitator had news from home that their father-in-law had passed away, so he needed to go home to support his family. While this left me on my own to run the event, I was still able to go ahead. It was too late to cancel the event as our participants were already arriving.

There have been many other examples where facilitators have dropped out at the last minute. The list of reasons is endless, but the result is the same. You can end up being one facilitator down. Having more than one facilitator can offer the option of carrying on the event or rescheduling. If there's only one facilitator, you have no choice but to cancel.

The challenging situations that are prevented by having a facilitator team

Having the support of other facilitators during an event helps to avoid many difficult situations. For example:

- Facilitator burnout

- Repeating the same mistakes that are hidden in your blind spots, e.g., ignoring some individuals and favoring others, going at the wrong speed for the group and either losing them or boring them

- Losing track of time. Consistent poor time management could result in severe overrun or missing other parts of the event to finish on time

- Not spotting challenging behavior. If you try to do everything, and the group is too big to manage on your own, pockets of unhelpful behavior may develop and quickly spread like a virus. By the time it is spotted, it may be too late

- Your facilitation style may not suit the group and irritate them

- If only one person is facilitating the event, they may tire as the event progresses. Progress may suffer as a result of the facilitator being tired. The energy in the room overall may drop as a result

The most prominent challenging situation to deal with if only one person is covering the event is absence. If you fail to show, the event may have to be canceled or rescheduled. Problems such as illness, travel delays, or human error can all lead to you not turning up. If a team is supporting the event and one person fails to show, you still have options.

SUMMARY OF PART I
THE ICEBERG

Prevention is better than cure (Proverb attributed to the Dutch philosopher Desiderius Erasmus). The amount of energy and stress required to recover a situation after it's happened is far higher than is needed to prevent it from occurring in the first place. By deploying the PREVENT checklist before an event, you will avoid most challenging situations.

Purpose

Prevent pointless meetings by having clarity on purpose and outcomes. Aligning everyone on what you're trying to achieve will guide you on the best way to succeed and who needs to attend.

Preventing pointless meetings will also prevent challenging behavior. How do you behave when you feel you're in a meeting that's wasting your time? Let the purpose guide you to the best way of achieving the desired outcome.

Resilience

Take care of yourself—mind, body, and soul. When you're tired and stressed, your ability to perform at your best will reduce. Your energy and enthusiasm may be limited, which can influence how much effort you invest in the rest of the PREVENT checklist.

Your mindset and behavior will impact how the group behaves. If you believe your group can achieve success, so will they. Resilience will help prevent difficult situations from occurring in the first place and escalation of problems when they do occur.

Focusing on adding value to your group will prevent you from doubting yourself and worrying about how you will look if things do go wrong. Your confidence will inspire others. Adopting a growth mindset will help to embrace challenges and deal with them more positively.

Environment

How does it feel in the room? Prevent initial anxiety from the group by making the room feel safe and welcoming. If you can give the impression that the group is in safe hands, they will be less challenging initially.

Prevent disruption during the event by having a social contract that supports everyone's needs, including yours. Agreeing upon boundaries for behavior can reassure the group that their experience will be a positive one.

Venue

Your venue could prevent your event from succeeding in three key areas:

- Location: Offsite venues prevent distractions and room hijacking. On-site venues prevent group anxiety from working somewhere different and disrupting their daily routines. Avoid working in open spaces of buildings if you can, as they are too distracting. Public areas offer poor safety and security for groups

- Size: Getting the right size room will prevent your group from feeling cooped up in cramped conditions or feeling lost and unheard in a vast space

- Layout: Choose a layout that will work for you and your group. The wrong one will prevent you from helping your group and effectively managing challenging behavior

Engagement

Prevent your group participants from being disengaged by building relationships and finding common ground among them. Getting your group to work on relevant topics and problems will prevent a disconnect between the event and reality. Move and mix people to keep things fresh. Working with the same people all day could create a stale experience.

Needs

Understanding the needs and context of your group can inform how you prime them. Priming can help prevent unpleasant surprises at the event, which could cause disruption and delay. Ensure you also prime the sponsor on what you need them to say and do to prevent the group from rejecting the event and its purpose. Ensure you're clear on what you need from the group and the Sponsor. You may also need to share any logistical needs with the organizer. Setting pre-work can get everyone prepared for the event and ready to contribute.

Team

Using a team to drive the event can prevent it from being canceled if one person drops out. Getting feedback from your team during the event will avoid the same mistakes being made again. Having a variety of people and styles facilitate the event can help prevent it from being boring.

PART II
THE SHIELD

INTRODUCTION TO PART II

Linking back to Chapter 2 (Resilience), knowing you don't need to have all the answers should boost confidence. Most facilitators feel comfortable when presenting content, especially if they've rehearsed. Dealing with questions can be a different matter. You can rehearse answers to some standard questions. However, you never know what questions will occur, and if you'll be able to answer them.

If it's a simple clarification question that requires a quick and easy answer, it makes sense to respond. For example, "How long have we got to complete the activity?" For all other questions, I recommend *not* answering them. Instead, get the group to answer their questions using the SHIELD strategies. There are six reasons for not answering questions:

1. Answering some questions and not others may allow your group to guess the extent of your knowledge. By

employing the SHIELD strategies consistently, your group won't know your knowledge limit.

2. Getting the group to answer any questions posed encourages them to think more. Engagement may increase as a result.

3. Encouraging the participants to answer any questions posed enables them to become more resourceful. Discovering their answers reduces their reliance on you.

4. When participants answer their questions, the ownership of the response (and any actions) rests with them. You don't want them blaming you when they don't like the answer. You also don't want to be the scapegoat if the action taken doesn't work out.

5. Not answering questions posed sends a signal to the group that you are not going to do all the work. For the event to be successful, they will also need to do some work.

6. If you decide to answer, some participants may begin to test how much you know by asking more challenging questions. They may think twice about this strategy if they know such requests will bounce back to them. The test of knowledge will then rest with the person asking the question.

If you're a facilitator, the focus should be on managing the process rather than contributing to the content. By answering content type questions, you will start to go beyond the purview of the facilitator. If you're a presenter delivering content, then there's an expectation of answering questions. You're the expert. A facilitator shouldn't have such pressure.

Getting the group to address their questions will ensure they focus on the content. Your focus is to manage the process of getting them to the desired outcome.

You can use each of the SHIELD strategies independently. However, for some questions, you may need to employ more than one approach. If so, you can work your way through them sequentially.

Typically, only one or two of the SHIELD strategies will be required to handle a challenging question. If you need more, there's a choice of six to select.

The six SHIELD strategies are:

- **S**pecify
- **H**and back
- **I**nvolve others
- **E**volve the question
- **L**ook or Leave
- **D**istract them with something else

Questions are good news!

As a facilitator and heeding growth mindset, questions from the participants are good news. Questions show that the group is engaged, thinking about the topic, and trying to understand more. Questions reveal what the group is interested in or worried about regarding the subject.

The number of people willing to respond provides insight into how valuable the question is in helping the group's overall understanding of the topic. It's okay if only a few people join in. It's worth checking with the group to see if the answers address the question. If not, keep asking for input from others. If the group feels satisfied with the responses already offered, move on.

Questions reveal what the group is interested in or worried about.

You do have to keep an eye on the time. Ideally, you will have built-in some time for questions in your plan. If there are no questions and you get some time back, the spare time can be used elsewhere in the event. Alternatively, you can give everyone a more extended break or even better, finish early!

CHAPTER 8
S – SPECIFY

Be more specific, please!

The first strategy that can help when dealing with a difficult question is Specify. You may not always need it, but it's the best place to start if a question feels vague. There are three elements to specify, and you can use any combination of them, depending on the question:

1. Narrow the scope of the question
2. Ask for an example
3. Clarify interest / concern

1. Narrow the scope of the question

I was once asked in a Project Management workshop, "How do you deal with poor performance?" It felt vague. There could have been many different answers. The question related to handling poor-performing personnel on the project team. Without specifying, the person asking would have been frustrated with solutions covering other aspects of poor performance on projects, e.g., schedule slippage. He would have either politely given up or rephrased the question to allow everyone to have another go at answering. The vagueness would consume valuable time.

By specifying, you can narrow down the answer required, which will save everyone time and effort. It also provides additional time for everyone to think about a more helpful response. In the example of poor performance, asking a question back, such as, "Can you help me understand what you mean by poor performance?" can quickly align everyone in the room on the definition of the phrase and its context.

Another example could be, "How do you motivate employees?" Most people will have different opinions on how to motivate employees. Vague questions can lead to unhelpful answers. By narrowing down the problem and asking, "Is there an aspect of employee motivation that you're interested in?" the questioner may start to explain what's driving the question. For example, "How can you motivate employees using non-financial incentives?" The additional information specifies the problem enough to help the group provide more targeted answers.

2. Asking for an example

Asking for an example can also help to understand the context behind the question. For instance, "We've tried implementing a change like this before and failed, what makes this time any different?" There are many assumptions in the question. Resist being dragged into defending why the initiative is different. Also, don't assume that the questioner is correct in their interpretation of previous attempts at change. A more helpful response to this would be, "Can you share an example of when implementing change failed?"

Clarifying will help get everyone in the room on the same page as the questioner. Responding by asking for an example will help remind everyone of a time when implementing change did fail. There may be an opportunity to explore lessons learned and avoid repeating the same mistakes. Also, the example will provide everyone in the room with a chance to validate how accurate the questioner's assessment is. Others may have different views of the case and the extent of success or failure.

The danger is starting a debate on previous attempts at change and relative success. Such a deviation will take time and detract from the focus on the current situation. However, if it helps the group learn from previous mistakes and inform how they will approach the current activity, it may be time well spent.

3. Clarify interest or concern

Clarify is subtly different from narrowing the scope of a question. Narrowing the scope of a question aligns everyone on the *what*. Clarify helps to surface *why* they are asking the question. Clarify also provides a chance to check what the person already knows.

In one example, no one had bothered to tell the group why they were at a training event I was running, including me. I had wrongly assumed the Sponsor had briefed the group before the event. As such, everyone was very suspicious about the event.

At the time, I didn't realize this. One person, Karl, asked, "What's this event all about?" It seemed a straightforward question about the agenda and objectives, so I answered it. Based on the continued frown and overall body language, Karl didn't seem satisfied and came back with a follow-up question. "Why am I here?"

The request seemed innocent enough. However, I resisted answering straight away. I clarified, hoping I could start to uncover the reason behind the question. I asked, "What do you know about the event?" He explained that no one had said anything about why he was attending.

Karl had assumed he was at the training as a remedial intervention. He felt he was attending as a punishment and that he's done something wrong. That began to explain his body language and general negative demeanor. I asked what the rest of the group knew about why they were here, and surprisingly, no one knew.

This example is where I learned about taking care of stakeholder needs and understanding the context surrounding an event (Chapter 6). I hadn't done any research on the event. I didn't understand the needs of the stakeholders, nor did I ask about the context.

In this instance, I was fortunate. I was about to leave the question until later when my co-facilitator (Michael) stepped in. He was a local leader and took on the matter. Michael explained that there was no money for promotions or pay increases. However, Michael knew the Sponsor wanted to invest in her top talent through training, which came from a different budget. This training was a reward for her top performers.

If you guess what's driving the question, you may not address the real need.

No one knew why they were at the event. I could tell by everyone's facial expressions and body language that they felt

S – SPECIFY

equally negative about being in the room. It wasn't only Karl. They all thought they were there as a punishment. Without Michael, I would have been forced to leave the question until a break.

As soon as Michael explained that everyone in the room was there as a reward, their mood improved. It improved even further when they realized they were regarded as top performers by their leader.

Clarifying a question can begin to address the underlying concern or interest behind an issue (*I've done nothing wrong, so why am I here to be punished?*). If you guess what's driving the question, you may not address the real need—*Why am I here? You're here to learn how to lead large teams.*

The danger in not answering a question is causing irritation and frustration in the group. The trade-off is not wasting everyone's time responding in a way that doesn't help the questioner and the group. Spending a few brief moments specifying the question will help the group focus on a more targeted answer that gives everyone a better learning opportunity.

TOP TIP

Try not to rate a question you get, for example, "That's a great question." The ratings you give may vary per person leading to alienation of those people whose questions were not highly rated compared to those who were. Very often, the initial reaction verbalized through judgment, and your facial expression gives away your delight or displeasure at a question. It's better to pause, breathe, think, and decide what appropriate response is required.

CHAPTER 9

H – HAND BACK THE QUESTION

What do you think is the answer?

Once a question is clear to everyone in the room, it is ready to be answered. As the facilitator, I recommend that you hand back the question rather than answering it. This chapter will look at how you can hand back a question to the person who is asking. If they're interested enough to raise the issue, they should have an opinion on the matter.

Hand back directly to the person asking the question

The person asking a question will usually have some insight into the answer, even if they may not yet be fully aware of it. Like coaching, the facilitator's role is not to solve problems and answer questions posed by the group. Instead, it is to

H - HAND BACK THE QUESTION

help the group navigate their way to their answers by helping unlock their potential resourcefulness. By doing this, the group participants are more likely to own the solution and any associated actions since they produced the answer.

For instance, in Chapter 8 (Specify), there was an example question about a previous attempt at implementing change. The person asking had a concern based on the failure of an earlier attempt at implementing change. Handing the issue back to the questioner enables everyone in the room (including the facilitator) to learn more about their experience. The new information may or may not inform the current situation.

Also, the questioner is concerned enough about the topic to raise the question. Handing the problem back to the person asking first allows them to explore the item further. There may be other people in the room who may not be as interested or concerned and, therefore, less likely to have a view.

TOP TIP

When someone is asking a question, watch for reactions from the rest of the group. The questioner may be embarking on a personal crusade and using the event as a platform to further their cause. If you notice the rest of the room, roll their eyes, which suggests that they're thinking, "Here we go again," be aware! Responding to the question to appease the questioner as the expense of consuming the whole group's time may not be the best course of action. Instead, it would be better to park the question and either come back to it later (if time allows) or deal with it offline in a break. See Chapter 12 - Leave it until later.

Assuming you have already specified the question, demonstrate that you have listened actively by summarizing your understanding. Play back the issue in your own words to check your clarity. Rephrasing the question in your own words also helps those in the room who haven't been paying attention. Involving others will be covered in Chapter 10.

Use open questions

Some questions posed may be evident and straightforward. For example, "Do you have any tips on how to prepare for a negotiation?" In such situations, it may not be necessary to specify. Instead, you can go straight to handing back the question. If so, when handing the item back, try to keep your response as short as possible. For example, "What tips do you have?" or, more generally, "What do you think?"

When you're handing questions back, phrase them as open questions rather than closed ones. A closed question requires a yes or no answer or specific data (e.g., *what time do we finish?*). An open question requires a more detailed response.

In the question of preparing for negotiations, handing back using a closed question such as, "Do you have any tips?" will give the questioner an easy way out. They could respond with a "no." Don't offer the questioner an easy way out; it makes you work harder to get an answer.

Handing back the question with an open question such as, "What tips do you have?" suggests that you're expecting the questioner to have an answer. Even if the answer is a guess or a perspective, it's a start. This approach sends a subtle signal to the rest of the group that if they ask a question, they will be the first ones invited to answer their question. Participants will think twice about asking questions attempting to trip you up.

TOP TIP

When someone contributes a response, and they speak very quietly, the temptation is to move closer to them and lean in. Being physically close to the responder naturally reduces their volume. Others in the group may not be able to hear what they're saying. If people can't listen to an answer, they may disengage from the topic. Alternatively, you may find yourself repeating the comment, which adds time and effort to the proceedings.

Instead, although counter-intuitive, use the space in the room to move away from the responder. The distance will require the responder to speak up, and everyone in the room will be able to hear. If people can hear, they will more likely remain engaged as well as being able to respond.

CHAPTER 10

I – INVOLVE THE REST OF THE GROUP

What does everyone else think the answer is?

You have specified the question. You have then moved on to give the person asking the question the chance to think and respond. If the answer from the person asking the question is enough, move on. If not, it's time to involve the rest of the group. This chapter looks at how to include the rest of the group.

It is often helpful to flush out views from the broader group to enhance the learning opportunity a question offers. It not only gives other people in the group a chance to add their perspective, but it also ensures that the overall engagement in the group remains high. When other people begin to add their perspective, the group starts to benefit from a range of diverse views. Let's continue using the example of the negotiations used in the previous chapter. When more group members respond with their tips, the rest of the group learn more about preparing for negotiations. Everyone begins to learn from each other's experiences.

How to involve the whole group

When handing back to the group, use short, open questions, such as, "What does everyone else think?" If you initially get a lot of blank looks from the rest of the group, there are some techniques you can quickly apply to get everyone back on the same page.

Summarize. There may be some micro nappers in the room (those people who have tuned out momentarily to think about something else). Quickly summarize the question and the answer provided so far. The only solution provided so far will be from the person asking the question.

Clarify. Having summarized, check that everyone understands the question. A closed clarification question requires a yes or no answer. If the answer is "no," then the rest of the group needs help. To rectify this, you will need to revert to the "Specify" strategy. Involve the person who asked the question initially to explain the problem to the group.

If the answer is "yes," and everyone else does understand, then someone else in the room should have a perspective to share, and you will need to be patient in finding them.

TOP TIP

Use the power of silence. In a group environment, most humans hate silence. Silence is most likely to occur when someone asks a question requiring someone to break the ice and provide an answer. When you ask a question, and you face a wall of silence, hold your nerve!

THE FEARLESS FACILITATOR

When you ask a question, and you face a wall of silence, hold your nerve!

Assuming you've checked that everyone understands the problem, remain silent. Count to at least twenty seconds (it will feel like a lifetime). There are more of them (participants) than you, and almost always, someone will crack to break the silence and provide an answer. Don't be tempted to fill the silence; otherwise, you will let the group off the hook. Do this a few times, and the group will know what's expected of them when a question comes.

Funnel. You can use the funneling technique to extract a response from others. Occasionally, even after twenty or thirty seconds of silence, no one else seems forthcoming with an answer. Don't panic! Use the funneling technique to get others engaged in answering the question. Hand back the question to the rest of the group and then gradually funnel down to more specific parts of the group. The funnel will vary on the room layout. Ultimately, you will be funneling down from the whole group to one half of the room, to a specific table team or row of individuals, to particular pairs or individuals. For instance:

- Select one half of the room

    "What do the people in the back half of the room think?"

- Select one row or table team

    "Back row/table team, talk to me. What do you think?"

- Select one or two individuals from the back row/table team

I – INVOLVE THE REST OF THE GROUP

"Chris, Robin, we've not heard from you in a while. What do you think?"

Each time you funnel down, use silence to allow someone in the new target group to come up with an answer. Someone will crack at the discomfort of prolonged silence, and as their apparent safety in numbers begins to dwindle, they will feel compelled to respond with an answer.

When you engage the funneling technique, try to do it with a smile because it can feel quite intimidating when your focus (and the focus of the rest of the group) begins to hone in on a smaller target group. You want the target group to feel the pressure but in a positive way. Smiling and softening your tone of voice can help achieve this because it will feel less threatening to engage.

TOP TIP

When asking the rest of the group a question, there is often no right or wrong answer, but different and equally valid perspectives. The question asking for tips on how to prepare for negotiations is a great example. Everyone who has experience of negotiations will have a valid perspective. Participants are often reluctant to answer for fear of getting it wrong and looking foolish in front of their peers. Reminding them that there are no right or wrong answers to the question and that every contribution is valid and helpful to the group can be very encouraging. This reminder will help maintain the psychological safety within the group.

The social contract may often include an entry that suggests there are no wrong suggestions or ideas. If such an entry exists on the contract, remind the group to encourage contributions.

THE FEARLESS FACILITATOR

Once you have a few more answers to the question, check with the questioner (and rest of the group) that the responses given address the question. Hopefully, it has, but if it hasn't, you will need to work with the group to decide if the question warrants more time spending on it or whether it's better to move on.

CHAPTER 11

E – EVOLVE THE QUESTION

Shall we discuss this or move on?

You have specified the question so that everyone understands it. You've also handed it back to the person who initially asked and received a response. Things are going well. Even better, the rest of the group has gotten involved. However, there's a problem. The topic has touched a nerve with the group and opened a Pandora's box of strong, diverse views. Unpacking and making sense of all the responses will require more time and energy than expected.

Occasionally during an event, there will be a topic that ignites either the whole group or most of them. They feel so passionately about the subject that they desperately want everyone to hear their perspective. You quickly realize this with the volume of voices trying to speak, the speed and tone of the responses, and the participants' body language.

Everyone's sitting up and actively engaged, desperate for their turn to speak. This chapter is about what you do next!

When faced with a barrage of participants wanting to contribute responses, you can tell that you've found a subject that is close to their hearts. In this chapter, we will look at helping the group choose what to do next. Choice gives the group a certain level of freedom and responsibility. Assuming the decision is to explore the question further, we will look at how you can turn the volume of responses into a structured learning discussion. By the end of the debate, there needs to be some form of conclusion and learning with relevant actions.

Do we need to spend more time on this?

When it becomes clear that most of the group wants to contribute to the question, it's a good idea to give them the choice of either spending more time on it or moving on. Having a clear agenda in the room and visible throughout the event (i.e., on a flip chart) can help the group review what's left to cover and make an informed decision. Ultimately, it's their event, and they should determine which topics to focus on to gain the most value from it. Also, giving the group the sense that they are in control of their destiny will ensure they remain engaged. If you begin to dictate and impose where you want to focus and remove some element of power from the group, you may experience some challenging behaviors. Some members of the group may start resisting your imposed control and direction.

Assuming the group decides they want to spend more time on the topic and are aware of any consequences of doing so (e.g., extending the event duration or dropping another agenda item), then evolving the question into a learning discussion is the next step. A learning discussion will allow the group to explore the topic in more detail. Providing them with some structure will enable you to lead the group through the discussion and reach a helpful conclusion. If you don't provide structure, the group will end up having an informative but unproductive, meandering chat.

Let the TALKS begin

There are five distinct phases to follow when facilitating a learning discussion. The phases will provide structure and guide you to a learning outcome, and they are:

T – Target, topic, and themes

A – Ask the group

L – Listen and learn

K – Key points

S – Summarize the learning

T – Target, topic, and themes

Target. To run a useful learning discussion, you need to think about what it's trying to achieve. What will be the learning outcome and the value to the group from spending time exploring the topic further? It's helpful to think about the target for the discussion—what are you aiming at? While defining the goal takes time, the discussion will be more focused and productive, thus saving time. Also, ensuring the defined outcome aligns with the question asked will help satisfy the group, who are intent on exploring the subject further.

Topic. To reach the target (learning outcome), you need to be clear on the scope of the discussion. What are the boundaries? If the topic is too broad, it will take a long time to reach the target. If the topic is too narrow, the amount of learning gained from the discussion may be limited. Ideally, you will have already defined the topic using the "Specify" strategy when the question was initially asked. Based on the volume and variety of responses from the group, you may feel further refinement of the topic is required. If in doubt, share your observations with the group and work with them to agree where the focus should be.

For example, when I run a Train-the-Trainer course, I often get asked, "Why run learning reviews?" This question usually follows straight after we've run a learning review. As it stands, the topic is vast and could go anywhere. It's hard to know what's driving the question at this stage, making it difficult to know what the learning requirement is.

By using the Specify strategy, I can get behind the question to narrow the scope and refine the topic to match the request. Typically, participants want to know what the value of running a learning review is. The group realizes it takes time and effort to set up and run them.

> **Think of the topic as a book title and the themes as chapters within that book. The target will be the learning gained from exploring the book.**

The topic for the discussion becomes, "To understand the value in conducting learning reviews." The target (learning outcome) is to decide whether learning reviews add value to an event or not. The learning will influence whether the students will include reviews into their future events.

Thinking about the target is vital at this stage because evolving the question into a discussion requires you to help the group reach a learning outcome from the initial question asked. Assisting the group to define the topic (scope) and clarify their target destination (learning outcome) is the first step. You can't guide the group unless you know where they want to go.

Themes. Themes will provide structure to the discussion. Think of the topic as a book title and the themes as chapters

E - EVOLVE THE QUESTION

within that book. The target will be the learning gained from exploring the book.

You may get a sense of the themes from the initial responses received in "Handing back the question" and "Involving others." After validating the topic and target with the group, clarify the themes (areas) to be explored in the discussion.

In the learning reviews example, participants often talk about reviews being valuable because of:

- Aiding memory recall
- Injecting fun into the event
- Providing an opportunity to work with different people

Memory recall, fun, and working with different people would be the three themes of the discussion, exploring the value of learning reviews. For each theme, cycle through the Ask, Listen and Learn, and Key points phases. Once all the themes have been covered, you can summarize the discussion and help the group determine what has been learned.

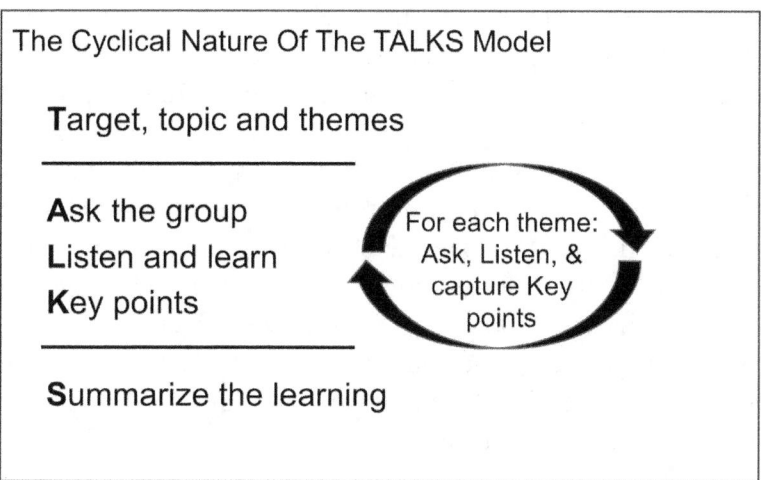

Chunking the discussion into themes (chapters) provides structure to help you and the group remember the input and manage the time. If there are lots of themes, check with the group about which ones should take priority in the discussion.

TOP TIP

Write the topic and target down where it's visible to everyone. Providing a helpful reference will help the group to remain focused. It also helps anyone just coming into the room to catch up with the rest of the group quickly. Capture the themes too, so everyone knows the flow. The visible themes will help when summarizing the discussion.

A. Ask the group

You have shared the topic with the group and checked with them that they understand it. You have identified and agreed on the target and which themes to focus on (assuming you had too many initial inputs to the question.)

Now it's time to move into the asking phase of TALKS. The group should start offering their views. Silence shouldn't be a problem. The group has already demonstrated its interest in the topic, with key individuals providing initial responses.

Warning! When you open the discussion and ask the group, be careful not to run a one-to-many model where you repeatedly ask the same question to different participants. Such repetition will not only slow everything down, but it will also become monotonous. It will potentially give you twenty different responses from twenty participants, making the discussion very wide and not very deep. As the facilitator, you will become a bottleneck as people funnel their responses through you for validation.

E - EVOLVE THE QUESTION

Instead, aim for an intragroup discussion dynamic where the group discusses amongst themselves, requiring only intermittent intervention from you. To do this, take the first theme and bounce it back to the group. For example, "Tom thinks that reviews are valuable since they help to recall learning. What does everyone else think about that?" You then spend time comparing and contrasting views amongst the group on that theme.

Other members of the group will hopefully begin to contribute based on their experiences of reviews. When different participants begin to share, the discussion will shift to an intra-group dynamic with you managing the process.

TOP TIP

When an intragroup dynamic develops in a discussion, it will gain momentum quickly, so you will need to be alert to what's being said and keep up!

L. Listen and Learn

As the facilitator, you need to pay attention throughout the discussion. Blink, and you will miss something, especially if the group is in the flow sharing contrasting experiences on the theme. Engaging your active listening skills, playing back what you've heard so far. The playback enables you to check your understanding of the input. Providing a quick summary also reminds the group of the progress made so far. For example, "While I've heard some of you say that fun is essential when reviewing learning because it increases energy and engagement, others have argued that fun dilutes the focus on recalling knowledge. Based on this, when does fun get in the way of reviewing learning?"

The group would then analyze the balance between having fun and reviewing learning. You don't have to summarize at the end of each person's input. However, it is helpful to notice where the group agrees and disagrees. Highlight the contrast in views to deepen the learning on the theme.

K. Key Points

When the group has explored a theme sufficiently, summarize what the key learning points are for it. Summarizing the key points will help close that theme (chapter) before moving onto the next one. It will also help you at the end of the discussion because you will have summarized each theme as it concluded, making recall easier. Keep in mind how the learning from each theme ties back to the target (learning outcome).

The danger in summarizing a theme is your ability to remember the key points. Recall becomes trickier if it's been a long discussion with lots of contrasting views. However, worrying about trying to remember points is often a self-fulfilling prophecy. While facilitating, you may find yourself pondering about potentially missing something. During your inner dialogue, you will inevitably do precisely that. If the pressure of trying to remember the key points is too much, you have three options.

Option one, which is my preferred option, is to get the group to do the recall and summary for you, e.g., "What have we learned regarding fun being valuable for learning reviews?" The person who started off the discussion is most likely to start since they mentioned the theme in the first place. You will notice that when someone does start the recall, your knowledge and recall will come flooding back, and you can fill in the blanks where required.

Option two is to capture some of the key points yourself on a flip as the discussion is taking place. There are hazards in multi-tasking. The first problem is that when you're writing, you are not listening. To avoid missing something, you will need to pause the proceedings while you capture the point. Halting a discussion can disrupt its flow.

The second problem is if you don't pause the discussion, you may miss what else is said. Very few people can remember and capture a point accurately while trying to keep up with an ongoing debate.

The third problem is that while writing, you lose eye contact with the group, and your ability to stay with the group deteriorates. In my experience, this is not a preferred option but an option, nevertheless.

Option three is to get a participant or co-facilitator to scribe at a flip chart and capture the key points for everyone. You can maintain focus with the group and keep up with the flow while still having a record visible on the key points. You will still need to summarize throughout to help the scribe capture each critical point accurately. If the writer captures everything, the flip will soon be full of text and hard for anyone to understand. Also, make sure you're using a different flip chart than the one containing the discussion topic and themes; otherwise, the group will lose their frame of reference.

Once you have summarized the key points of the first theme, move onto the next, and repeat the Ask, Listen, and Key points steps.

How many themes and key learning points?

The short answer is between five and nine learning points. There may be a varying number of learning points per theme.

George A. Miller, a pioneer in Cognitive Psychology, discovered that human short-term memory is generally limited to holding seven pieces of information, plus or minus two.[18] Therefore, the sweet spot for individuals retaining learning in their short-term memory is between five and nine key learning points.

Some discussions are more in-depth than others. A topic may only have one or two themes that need exploring in depth. The depth covered in each theme may generate several learning points.

Other discussions may be broader and contain three to five themes. If so, each theme should generate one to two learning points. Remember, short-term memory can retain five to nine pieces of information.

Also, keep in mind your time management. If there are any more than five themes, the discussion will take too long. Some members of the group will start to lose interest and become restless. It will also make it much harder to recall the learning of several themes.

S – Summarize the learning

Summarizing the learning will confirm if the target for the discussion has been met. Even if the participants have learned something useful from the discussion, there's more work to do. My favorite question to ask after any learning intervention is, "So what?" In the discussion about learning reviews, the group learned about the value of reviews, but so what? What are the participants going to do with that learning? Translating the knowledge into tangible, meaningful actions will begin to address the question of "So what?" The discussion summary will help answer the question.

By breaking the discussion into themes, you can cover the learning using the key points from each theme. You can use the same options to do the summary, as you did when summarizing the key points. You can summarize yourself, get the participants to do it, or ask your scribe.

Three questions which can help the participants make the shift from the general learning of the discussion to them specifically are:

E - EVOLVE THE QUESTION

a) What did you learn?

b) What are you going to do with your learning?

c) When are you going to do it?

The participants are unlikely to act on all the learning points from the discussion. Some points will resonate more than others. Which points resonate with participants will vary depending on their background, experience, and knowledge base. The three summary questions help make the shift from the general learning of the discussion to each participant's context and needs.

Therefore, ensure you allow time for the group to reflect and capture their learning points from the discussion. Giving time to reflect can help translate the learning into possible action and application. If there's no time to reflect, the learning and any potential actions may be lost.

If you have plenty of time, get the participants to pair up, share, and refine their learning and actions. If the pair agree to check in with each other regularly to monitor progress, the likelihood of each person completing their actions goes up significantly.

It's even better if you have time to get the participants to share one of their actions with the whole group. Listening to others' actions may spark an additional idea in someone else.

Don't sacrifice the Summary!

If, during the discussion, you notice time is running short, I recommend being transparent with the group about time and giving them a choice to continue or move on. If time is short and the group agrees, it is better to reduce the number of themes covered in the discussion rather than sacrifice the Summary. Prioritizing the themes at the start enables the most important ones to be addressed first. The group may be willing to drop the lower priority themes to save time.

Investing time in making sense of what the value has been from the discussion in terms of learning and actions will outweigh the benefit of covering another theme. If you miss out on the Summary, you will leave people wondering what the value of the discussion was. The "so what?" will remain unanswered.

As humans, we like closure; we need to know how a story ends. A discussion without a summary will be frustrating because of the lack of closure. The group will feel cheated. They've committed time and effort participating in the discussion but didn't get an ending. It's like watching a movie and being asked to leave the cinema twenty minutes before the end.

> **A discussion without a summary will be frustrating because of the lack of closure.**

If the group is getting value from the discussion, they may want to continue with the agreed themes. However, they will need to accept the consequences of sacrificing something else from the agenda or finishing later. I have learned over the years that if the group is getting value from a discussion, they won't let you move on until they are ready to do so.

The benefit of following the TALKS process is the cyclical nature of the Ask, Listen/learn, and Key Points phases. If you need to move on due to time pressure or group fatigue, you can step out of the A-L-K cycle after discussing the current theme and close with the Summary.

A final thought on learning discussions

Evolving a question into a learning discussion is a tough decision. It will take time and effort from you and the group to explore a topic in more depth. Let the group guide you by

E - EVOLVE THE QUESTION

providing them with a choice. The topic may be unsolvable and offer little value in being discussed. If the group chooses to explore further, giving structure to enable them to gain insight will help manage the discussion and time.

CHAPTER 12

L – LOOK OR LEAVE

Shall we look at the question differently or leave it until later and move on?

You have specified, so everyone has clarity on the question. Despite handing back to the person asking the question and involving the rest of the group, no one in the room has an answer. You've exhausted the first three SHIELD strategies (Specify, Hand back, Involve). You're unable to evolve the topic further because no one has responded. Now what?

This chapter will explore two options available when the group seems unable to respond to a question raised.

First, it will consider how viewing the topic from a different perspective can shift energy and promote thought.

Second, this chapter will also explore the reality that sometimes it's better to leave a question until later. There may not be the right people in the room or the necessary data to provide an appropriate response.

Look at the question another way

The first option of the "Look or Leave" strategy is to look at the question another way. For example, in one project kick-off workshop, one of the clients asked me, "How are you going to make this project a success?" As the Project Manager brought in to run the project, I wanted to know the client's thoughts on project success. I handed back the question to the client who asked. He responded, "You're the management consultants; you tell me!" I tried involving the rest of the clients in the question to see what thoughts they had on project success. All I got back was a wall of silence and a higher than average count of clients folding their arms looking decidedly unimpressed.

The question was too important to leave and move on since it was clear the clients were expecting an answer. I believed the right people were in the room to find a solution. I wanted their input, so I got the clients to look at the question another way. I asked them, "What could we do to screw this project up?" After seeing some initially puzzled looks, the room erupted with noise. Everyone had a story to tell on previous project disasters that they were involved in during their careers. I captured some key themes, such as lack of stakeholder buy-in, poorly defined benefits, poorly managed scope, insufficient budgets, and resources.

I then ran a learning discussion about how we would avoid those potential causes of project failure, which ultimately led to how we would deliver a successful project.

The same technique can be employed if your group is stuck with a current problem and isn't able to move on. Rather than focusing attention on the apparently insolvable current problem (e.g., this company is in a mess, how would you fix it?), ask the group to look at the question differently. Shift the focus from the current problem to describing an ideal future. Once they've done that, work backward from the future state to the current situation.

Groups can often get stuck in the present and can't see beyond it, sapping energy. Shifting their energy and focus on a future state releases their creativity. When doing this, get the group to paint a picture as vivid as possible to see where they want to go. Boosting creativity and energy will generate the momentum needed to help the group work back from their ideal state to their current problem.

If the question relates to other stakeholders, e.g., customers, asking the group to view the problem as a customer may help shift the thinking. Looking at an issue from another person's perspective can generate empathy. The group may be looking at the problem logically from their viewpoint. Stepping into the shoes of someone else and experiencing the issue from their perspective can often be the catalyst needed to find an answer.

Providing your perspective

Another way of looking at the question is by providing your view. Wherever possible, try to resist the temptation to offer an answer. However, it remains an option when the group is stuck. As stated in the introduction to SHIELD, answering questions for the group will make them less resourceful and more reliant on you as the facilitator. Providing answers can create more problems for you later because the group becomes wise to the prospect of you bailing them out of dealing with tough questions.

Your knowledge and experience of the subject matter may enable you to provide a perspective rather than giving a definitive answer. Offering a view may ignite a shift in thinking

L – LOOK OR LEAVE

amongst the group, thereby unlocking a solution to the question. If you do this, provide your perspective, and hand it back to the group. For example, "Based on my experience, when I've faced this type of situation, I did the following." Once you've finished relating your experience, follow up with, "How does that perspective fit with this situation?"

The danger with this tactic is the group coming back and saying, "Yes, we've tried that, and it didn't work." The group now expects you to produce another suggestion. All eyes are on you to rescue the group from the question. You've put the pressure of finding a solution onto yourself.

If providing your perspective ignites the group to think differently, then it's worth taking the risk. You can then continue involving the rest of the group or evolve the question using TALKS framework. If the group rejects your view and expects more suggestions from you, there's another option. Leave the problem until later.

The question falls into the *too difficult* bucket

As stated at the start of this chapter, you've exhausted the first three SHIELD strategies (Specify, Hand back, Involve), and because no one has the answer, you've been unable to Evolve the question any further. An alternative option in the Look or Leave SHIELD strategy is to leave the matter until later. Leaving it could mean either waiting until the end or addressing it after the event.

Having the agenda visible will help you to ask the group what they want to do. They can refer to the schedule and make an informed decision on how best to spend the remaining time at the event. The participants should be able to prioritize once they know what's left to cover. It will depend on the importance of the question and the other priorities identified on the agenda.

TOP TIP

If the group decides to leave the question until later, capture it on a "Parking Lot" flip chart and place it close to the agenda. The "Parking Lot" is a visual reminder that there is an outstanding item needing attention at a later point.

When placing an unanswered question in a "Parking Lot," it is recommended to spend a minute or so agreeing with the group about what they specifically want to do with the question. Options include:

- If there's time, come back to it at the end of the event
- Leave it until someone can find the relevant person or data during the event
- Address it after the event

The group may decide to leave it until the end of the event, but this rarely works, in my experience. By the end of the event, the group is typically exhausted and in no mood to tackle something they couldn't deal with earlier.

Please don't give up hope because occasionally, I have seen groups come back at the end to resolve a challenging question successfully. Other agenda items covered have informed and unlocked a solution to the problem. Addressing a problematic question may also be possible if you have a co-facilitator or a willing volunteer from the group. The volunteer can step out and find the missing stakeholder or information that will help tackle the problem.

If it's clear that no one in the room has an answer to the question and coming back to it later won't make any difference, it's best to leave it until after the event.

L – LOOK OR LEAVE

TOP TIP

Highlight any remaining items on the "Parking Lot" at the end. I recommend spending a few minutes agreeing with the group who has the action to follow up on an item after the event. Agree on a timeline for the work to increase accountability on the outstanding question.

Knowing there is an option to leave the matter and move on will give you confidence when the group becomes stuck.

CHAPTER 13

D – DISTRACT THEM WITH SOMETHING DIFFERENT

What's this I'm now showing you? It looks interesting!

This chapter will explore the final SHIELD strategy. It will look at how to distract the group with something else to move on subtly. It may appear to be cowardly, moving away from something too difficult to solve. The intention is honorable in helping the group move onto something which adds value to them. The chapter will explore some of the ways you can distract a group without them feeling cheated. Some methods are more subtle than others, but the result will be the same.

Ideally, by deploying the other SHIELD strategies effectively, you should not need to resort to this final strategy. However, if the group becomes bogged down by a question, moving on could be the best course of action.

D – DISTRACT THEM WITH SOMETHING DIFFERENT

Groups can get bogged down when a question is more substantial than they can handle, e.g., above their pay grade. Another example is where the group only wants to moan about something beyond their control, e.g., a change in company policy. There will be limited value spending more time on the question because the right people aren't in the room to solve it.

When the group becomes stuck, the previous strategy of "Leaving it" and placing it in the "Parking Lot" should be enough. Occasionally, some members of the group will fancy an opportunity to vent their frustration, knowing there is no possibility of solving the problem. These people feel justified consuming more time at the event by their need to vent and feel better.

There are some benefits to letting the moaning play out. Allowing people to get their issues off their chest can feel liberating. Once freed from their burden, participants often engage. The danger is alienating the other group members who generally simply want to move on rather than wait for their colleagues to feel better.

If you have already deployed the Leave SHIELD strategy and received consensus from the group to move on, but you can't because of a remaining few people who refuse to let go, there is more you can do. There are three options to move on when a minority is still actively moaning:

1. Suggest an impromptu break
2. Show the group something more interesting
3. Build ELMO into the Social Contract

1. Suggest an impromptu break

The first and easiest option is to suggest an impromptu break. A break will allow the group as a whole to take a breather and to reset the energy. Those who have disengaged from the debate will gladly get up and take advantage of the break.

Those who are still going will then have a choice. The minority can either continue their debate or give up and take a break. Either way, you and the rest of the group are free. The physical shift required to move towards coffee is often enough to snap the "gripers" out of their vicious circle. Regardless, a break is usually enough to move everyone on with minimal fuss.

2. Show the group something more interesting

The second option is more covert and requires a degree of luck, depending on where you are in the event agenda. Simply put, it's about giving the group something to look at, which distracts them and tempts them to move on.

The distraction could be showing a new slide or revealing a fresh new topic. It could be a handout which requires reading something rather than listen to the griping. It could be turning over a flip chart or revealing a poster.

The distraction aims to capture the attention of the group. It's a subtle way of saying to the group, "I'm ready to move on, are you?" The luck required is having something to show the group if you find yourself in this position. If not, there's a third option.

3. Build ELMO into the Social Contract

The third option is something called ELMO. ELMO stands for **E**nough! **L**et's **M**ove **O**n. I recommend building ELMO

D - DISTRACT THEM WITH SOMETHING DIFFERENT

into the Social Contract, so that everyone in the room is familiar with the term and how to use it.

Anyone can use ELMO. When anyone feels that enough time has been spent on a topic and thinks it's appropriate to move on, the contract allows them to call out "ELMO." The objective is to bring everyone back on track with the event agenda.

When someone shouts ELMO, you can then check around the room to see what the group's consensus is. Does the rest of the group agree with the call? The benefit of incorporating ELMO into the social contract is peer pressure. A request to move on is usually more impactful and accepted by the group if they initiate it rather than you.

Nothing is stopping you from using the term as well. If you think the group is going nowhere with the question, they will probably appreciate the gesture, agree with you, and move on.

TOP TIP

The willingness of participants to call out at an event within a group varies across cultures. I recommend checking what's acceptable behavior locally first. If it's okay, then introduce ELMO at the beginning of the event and get buy-in from the group to use it. Despite initial reservations, I know many people have felt liberated when invoking ELMO. They have spared time for themselves and their colleagues. Many are grateful to those few who dare to use ELMO.

Warning! Make sure ELMO is not being abused by some group members trying to shut down others when they have a valid point. As the facilitator, it's a judgment call hence the advice to check-in with the group when invoking ELMO.

SUMMARY OF PART II

THE SIX SHIELD STRATEGIES

Knowing that there are six SHIELD strategies to call upon when faced with a challenging question should provide the confidence to tackle whatever question comes your way.

Specify to narrow the scope of the question. Ask for a specific example to understand the context behind the subject. Clarify and explore what's behind the request. Answering the question at face value may not help.

Hand back the question to the person asking it. If they feel it's important enough to ask, they are more likely to have an opinion on the matter. It also sends a signal to the group that while asking questions is good, thinking about an answer is even better.

Involve the rest of the group. It may be helpful to seek more opinions on the question. Soliciting more responses and building consensus on the answer will help the group move forward.

THE SIX SHIELD STRATEGIES

Evolve the question into a learning discussion. By involving the rest of the group, there may be differing opinions that are worth exploring further. Agree on the topic (scope of the discussion) and target the learning (the goal of the discussion) before identifying some key themes to explore, which will enable the group to reach the target. Explore each topic theme by asking for views and listening/learning what the group thinks about each theme. Capture the key points of each theme before moving on to the next theme. Summarize the learning of the whole discussion at the end to reach the learning goal (target).

Look at the question another way if the group gets stuck. Explore different perspectives to shift their thinking. If that fails, **Leave** the question until later. Give the group a choice to move on or stick with the problem.

Distract the group with something else to do or look at if there's no value in carrying on. If a minority of the group can't let the question go or the whole group starts moaning, "Distracting" them may be helpful. Offering a break or something new to look at or do will distract. Encourage the group to use ELMO and leverage peer pressure to move on if required.

PART III
THE SWAN

INTRODUCTION TO PART III

To recap, you've done as much as you can to avoid challenging situations from occurring by following the PREVENT checklist. You've got six SHIELD strategies ready to deploy when challenging questions arise. The only other potential danger area facing you at your event is challenging behavior from your group.

Challenging behaviors can surface for a variety of reasons. A person may be having a bad day and bringing their mood to the event with them. Merely being in the room could be irritating for some people, having their regular schedule disrupted. There could be a clash of personalities sitting close together. There may be participants who simply don't get on and spend their time antagonizing each other.

Whatever the behavior, as a facilitator of an event, you will have to decide how best to deal with it as it occurs.

The first chapter in part three will look at how to determine what action to take. We will walk through a structured thought process to assess what action will best address the situation. Creating a delay in responding to behavior by going through a thought process will help prevent an automatic and potentially unhelpful reaction.

The remaining chapters will provide examples of intervention strategies. There are three intervention levels, each one having a dedicated chapter. The three levels of intervention—Green, Amber, and Red—represent the effort required to deploy an intervention. Green strategies need a light touch to address the behavior. Red strategies need lots of thought and energy mixed with careful handling of the situation. Amber strategies fall somewhere in between. There will be three to four intervention strategies to choose from at each level.

There will be a short description of each strategy, how it's applied, and which challenging behaviors it would best suit.

This third section likens a facilitator to a swan when faced with challenging behavior. The frantic energy expelled by the swan underwater is similar to the facilitator's mental effort when facing challenging behavior. As with the swan above the waterline, the facilitator needs to display a calm exterior appearance.

> **As with the swan above the waterline, the facilitator needs to display a calm exterior appearance.**

Remaining calm can be hard while thinking about what to do and trying to control your emotions.

I would like to offer some reassurance on challenging behaviors. Most of the time, the people I get to work with are fantastic. My wife, Emma, has stopped asking how the group was when I get home after an event because ninety-nine percent of the time, I give the same answer. The group was terrific. They were engaged, motivated, and kind. Would the groups be as cooperative if I didn't put all my energy and enthusiasm into facilitating an event? Who knows? I haven't yet dared to put this theory to the test. Generally, your participants don't wake up and decide that they will behave like jerks for the whole day. Something happens to them along the way, which causes challenging behavior.

CHAPTER 14

THINK BEFORE ACTING

Engage brain before opening mouth

Many years ago, I was running a Leadership Development training event for senior consultants. Generally, it was a well-behaved group. It was a three-day event with lots of content and activities to run through. However, right from the start, it was clear that one individual was not happy. It wasn't clear what the problem was. When she introduced herself, she used negative words, spoke in a monotone voice, and displayed closed body language (eyes down, folded arms).

I initially felt empathy for her. Perhaps she was shy or was having a rough week. The event ran from Wednesday to Friday. She could have been with clients earlier in the week. Sometimes clients give consultants a hard time when they disappear for training. At first, I chose to ignore it. I thought she would come around once she understood more about the course and its objectives. Also, I hoped that getting to know some of her more positive colleagues might help her mood.

However, as the first day unfolded, Ann's (not her real name) behavior got progressively worse. While she would not offer up any answers to questions posed, she would seek to disagree with anyone who did offer up a point of view. Also, she regularly challenged the content I was sharing. "Where's the evidence?" she would ask. "I think you're wrong," she would say. Even some of the most forceful personalities came under attack during the day.

I made the mistake of pandering to Ann's behavior. I failed to address it early on, and because of that, the situation deteriorated. Day one felt painful; each module generated one or two mini-battles between Ann and the rest of the group with me in the middle. I was hoping it would sort itself out on day two. Either Ann would feel a lot better having vented for most of day one or even better, Ann wouldn't show up. I was wrong.

Ann arrived on day two and was even angrier and more disruptive than on day one. I couldn't believe it. It was as if her mission was to sabotage the whole event for everyone. She had nothing positive to say and continued to challenge anyone's point of view on every topic.

I'd had enough and decided to confront Ann during the next break. I tried pointing out the impact her behavior was having on the group. She argued back that my observation was incorrect and that everyone appreciated her input. My mouth was wide open at this point, totally stunned at her reaction. I quickly recovered. I then asked Ann if she would try to interrupt less and let others speak more. I pointed out it would help the group to hear more views around the room. She accused me of attempting to sideline her, which pushed her from being angry to furious.

After apologizing that I wasn't attempting to sideline her, I asked if the course was right for her and if she was getting value from it. Ann simply shrugged her shoulders and said, "Let's see." She turned around and headed off into the classroom. It was a poor attempt at confronting the situation.

It got so bad that no one dared to contribute to questions being asked or offered an opinion in a learning discussion. The fear of incurring the wrath of Ann was too much for most people. The group had shut down. The situation reached its finale when I began ignoring Ann and her challenges. I think I got away with it once, but when I ignored her again, she exploded. It wasn't my proudest moment. Ann started shouting and screaming at me, saying how rude I was.

She grabbed her things and stormed out of the room. I quickly suggested an impromptu break to try to sort things out. There was no sign of Ann. As part of my event preparation, I had spoken to the Sponsor (Peter) about context and the participants' needs. He worked in the same building as the event, so I used the break to find him and explain what had happened. I brought Peter up to speed on the situation. He smiled reassuringly and told me not to worry. He knew about Ann and would speak to her. He said that she wasn't happy in her role. Ann did leave the Company two months later.

When everyone came back together after the break, it was though a thunderstorm had passed. The noise of the thunder and heavy rain of Ann had cleared to be replaced by a clear blue sky of calmness and serenity. The mood of the room changed in an instant from pessimism to optimism. People started speaking up again, even laughing when someone shared a funny story about their experience on a topic we were discussing.

My first learning from this story relates to my feelings. For too long, I was unwilling to tackle the situation. I was fearful of making things worse by attempting to address the problem. In the end, I was angry at Ann's behavior, which led to me ignoring her. My emotions got in the way of me making the right choices.

My next learning is how my behavior influenced Ann's. I pandered to her initial disruptions. Was this seen as acceptance by Ann? In the end, my frustration and anger leaked out by ignoring Ann. My behavior caused Ann to explode and walk out.

> **Appeasing a challenging behavior isn't an effective intervention strategy.**

My final learning relates to the impact on the group. Appeasing a challenging behavior isn't an effective intervention strategy. My reluctance to deal with Ann's behavior had limited the whole group's learning for nearly two days. It was my responsibility to deal with it, and I had chosen to ignore it. I felt like I had let the group down. No one was learning anything other than how annoying Ann was. I had hoped the situation would sort itself out, but it only got worse.

The experience of dealing with Ann caused me to re-think how I deal with challenging behavior. The result is the structured thought process covered in this chapter. It will look at three key questions to work through to help determine an effective intervention.

Whether you wish to implement action to address a behavior will depend on the answers to the three questions in the thought process. There is a balance to be struck. On the one hand, you don't want to be facilitating an event that feels like a dictatorial regime where there is zero-tolerance for challenging behavior. The group won't appreciate such control. On the other hand, you don't want to be running an event where anything goes, and chaos ensues.

You can achieve a better balance by starting with subtle, Green interventions. If the behavior continues, work your way up through Amber and Red until you resolve the situation.

Three Questions to Ask Yourself

When you observe challenging behavior, it can evoke many emotions within you. To avoid any unhelpful knee-jerk reactions, forcing yourself to go through a structured thought process can allow you some time to decide upon a more helpful intervention. Although this thought process may seem time-consuming on paper, going through this in real-time should only take a few seconds. Like counting to ten, you're building a buffer between reaction and response. Typically, counting to ten is aimed at calming you down. It prevents an escalation to the situation caused by your heightened emotional state. The difference here is that you're using the time productively to think about a response that will help you and the rest of the group. The three key questions to ask yourself in this buffer time are:

1. How does the challenging behavior make me feel?
2. What might be going on with the individual displaying the behavior?
3. What's the impact on the group and the consequences of letting the behavior continue?

1. How does the challenging behavior make me feel?

Most challenging behaviors can provoke an emotional reaction in you, which is why the first question addresses your feelings. It forces you to come to terms with whatever prevailing emotion you're experiencing. To get past the emotion, you first need to acknowledge it. It could be anger, frustration, disappointment, resentment, bitterness, or other unhelpful feelings. Once you've recognized the emotion, it's also helpful to understand what's driving it. How much of that feeling is fact-based, and how much comes from unsubstantiated assumptions?

Conflicting values

Negative feelings can arise when someone's behavior doesn't match your own set of core values and beliefs. For example, I hate being late. I think lateness shows disrespect to others who may be waiting for me. So, when participants are late for an event, I use the thought process to avoid chastising the individual in front of the group. The person may have a perfectly valid reason for being late. I simply don't know what it is yet.

Feeling threatened

Negative feelings can also arise when we feel threatened in some way. Challenging behavior may feel like an attempt to undermine your authority. You may feel your reputation as a capable facilitator is under threat.

Challenging behavior also has the potential to disrupt the event, taking it off track. You still feel threatened. The threat now relates to your agenda and timings. Our brains are always on the lookout for threats. As covered in Chapter 2, if we feel threatened, the amygdala part of our brain can take over. We no longer have access to the more rational prefrontal cortex. The amygdala will invoke a fight or flight response, often prompting an unhelpful reaction.

Going through the thought process will buy you the time needed to reduce the effects of the amygdala. Being able to access the prefrontal cortex will enable a more helpful response to be found. Being aware of your feelings and acknowledging them is the first step. Understanding where those feelings are coming from heightens your self-awareness and helps you to move on.

2. What might be going on with the individual displaying the behavior?

There may be a perfectly valid reason for a person to be displaying challenging behavior. Until you know for sure what that reason is, it's hard to make an intervention that feels appropriate to address the behavior. Three techniques can help here:

- Get curious, not furious
- Separate the behavior from the person
- Check that you are not causing the challenging behavior

Get curious, not furious

Finding out the reason for the challenging behavior will take time and effort. Depending on the situation, you may need to take the person aside to discuss it privately. When you're facing challenging behavior, you may not have the luxury of investigating at that moment in time. Instead, developing one or two possible rational reasons will help to reduce the internal threat level. Usually, there is a perfectly valid reason for the behavior. Until you have the chance to discover what's going on, get curious, not furious.

One experience I had illustrates how a lack of knowledge can lead to forming unhelpful conclusions. During one of my client projects, I initiated a Monday afternoon status meeting with the team leads from both the consulting and the client-side. There were six people in total. The meeting was always at three o'clock, which I felt was a reasonable time for everyone to make. There was one lady (Carol) from the client-side who rarely showed up to the meetings. When Carol was there, she rarely contributed. She kept any responses to questions short. It looked like Carol didn't want to be there. I felt she disrespected me as the project manager and that she wasn't committed to the project. I was going to escalate the situation to her Manager, but something inside me told me that would only make matters worse.

I decided the best course of action was to remain curious and talk to her about it. It turned out that Carol was a working mother who was juggling work and parenthood. Her husband dropped off the kids at school every morning, enabling her to come to work for 7 a.m. She needed to pick her kids up from school at 3.30 p.m. The commitment required her to leave work at 3 p.m. exactly as my meeting was due to start.

Get curious, not furious.

I didn't know Carol that well, so I had no idea about her kids. I had wrongly assumed the meeting time was convenient for everyone, and I hadn't bothered to check with them.

All the stories I was telling myself about Carol not respecting me and not being committed to the project were simply not true. From that experience, I learned the importance of getting to know my meeting attendees better and sooner. I also learned that sometimes, what appears to be challenging behavior is simply folks trying to deal with their problems. It's rare for someone to be deliberately trying to sabotage your event. In the end, I moved the meeting to 11 a.m., and everyone attended with no further problems.

TOP TIP

Start from a mindset of curiosity, wondering what's driving the behavior. You will more likely arrive at an intervention that can de-escalate or dissolve the situation. If you start from a mindset of paranoia (assuming everyone's out to disrupt your event), the response will be less helpful.

Separate the behavior from the person

It's essential to separate the behavior from the person. If you genuinely believe that the person displaying the challenging behavior is good, seeing their humanity will help you tailor your response more helpfully. There have been plenty of well-intentioned people attending my events whose actions haven't quite matched their intentions. One example of such behavior was David. He was passionate about the topic we were discussing. He wanted to help the whole group by sharing his knowledge. David didn't realize that he kept interrupting others who were trying to speak and contribute. He intended to help the group get to the same level of understanding as him. In reality, he ended up irritating the rest of the group.

There are many reasons which could be driving challenging behavior. Some people may be fearful of change, worried about their jobs, irritated by being forced to attend an event, frustrated at how things are progressing, or scared at making a wrong decision that will affect those around them.

Whatever the reason behind the behavior, try to maintain respect for the person. Recognize their humanity. The person will have feelings, wants, and needs.

If you can appreciate them as a person rather than focus on their irritating behavior, you are much more likely to behave in a respectful way. Remember, very few people will wake up in the morning and say to themselves, "Today, I think I'll behave like a jerk!" Something happens to them along the way, causing a deterioration in mood.

TOP TIP

Maintaining a healthy relationship with each participant is the key to facilitating successful events, and the only way to do this is to see them as well-intentioned good people. Give them the benefit of the doubt until proven otherwise.

If you don't see the person as a good person, and you begin to display signs of irritation like I did when I started to ignore Ann, the challenging behavior is likely to continue or deteriorate.

Does challenging behavior start with me?

The challenging behavior you're observing may be a symptom caused by you. Shifting the focus from the alleged guilty participant back to you will lead to a different response compared to the original one. In Chapter 2 (Resilience), we covered how your mood and behavior may be driving an unhelpful reaction in some of the participants. If you're tired, hungover, or worried about how the event will go, you may be susceptible to your negative thoughts and behaviors. If you look and sound like you don't want to be at the event because of any mental or physical fatigue or stress, it will show. The group could react to that by having thoughts like, "If our facilitator can't be bothered, why should we?"

Think back to the last time you had the misfortune of listening to a very dull presenter. Those sessions can feel painfully long. The offending presenter has no idea of their negative impact on the group. In the end, you'll often hear the presenter saying the group was a tough crowd. They are entirely unaware that it was their behavior that caused the crowd to be as tough as they perceived them to be. We are often blind to our shortcomings and find it much easier to blame the group for any lack of success at the event.

Here's a list of things to look out for which may indicate the source of the challenging behavior lies with you:

- You focus on some participants and ignore others
- You wish you were somewhere else
- You don't make eye contact with the group

- You use a monotone voice or mumble
- You dismiss input from participants
- You use humor or sarcasm which could feel inappropriate to members of the group
- You use offensive language
- You express a strong opinion about a topic to the group, which clashes with participants' views

There are many more ways your behavior will affect the group, which will spark challenging behavior in some participants. Remain open to the possibility that the source of the problem might be you!

3. What's the impact on the group and the consequences of letting the behavior continue?

You've controlled your emotions and engaged your prefrontal cortex to develop a rational response. You've got an idea as to what might be going on with the person displaying the behavior. Now it's time to think about the broader impact on the group. What could happen if the behavior continues?

Impact on the group now

Occasionally, there may be challenging behavior in the room, which affects you, but the rest of the group seems unaffected by it. What seems unacceptable to you appears okay to the group. If the behavior doesn't seem to be affecting the group and their progress, relax. No action is required, yet.

The behavior could be isolated, with only one person displaying the behavior. The impact on the group can vary. At one extreme, you may have someone doodling. The doodler may have no effect on the event except causing a minor distraction to those around them. On the other extreme, you may have one person like Ann, who causes mayhem and impacts everyone.

If challenging behavior is widespread, the impact on the group is likely to be higher. People wandering in and out of the room is a great example. Not only is the volume of movement distracting, but it can also impact group dynamics and focus. If the problem is widespread, it's best to tackle it early to stop it from spreading further.

Consequences

The consequences of letting behaviors continue will vary. Allowing the doodler to continue may encourage others around them to do the same. Very soon, a whole table group may be doodling or checking their phones. When I allowed Ann, the disruptor, to continue, it resulted in the group shutting down and disengaging completely.

In the rare situation where challenging behavior doesn't seem to impact the group, there will still be consequences. For example, in one Leadership Development workshop that I led, the leaders kept wandering in and out of the room to take calls. It seemed acceptable to the group since everyone seemed to be doing it throughout the first session. The consequence was that some missed essential decisions made in the room. When they found out about the decision, some of the absent leaders disagreed with it. The group had to revisit the decision to achieve consensus, costing them valuable time. We soon discussed being present and revised the social contract.

Another example is where the group is working in small parties. If folks are missing, the consequence is that some groups won't have enough people to work on an activity.

Very often, challenging behavior will have a distracting impact on the rest of the group. The consequence of not dealing with challenging behavior often leads to a ripple effect, impacting others, and creating an even more challenging situation. Assessing how the group is affected currently can indicate the severity of consequences later. If you choose not to act, I recommend keeping an eye on how things develop.

CHAPTER 15

GREEN INTERVENTION STRATEGIES

Green for "Gently does it!"

Going through the thought process discussed in the previous chapter should help determine which intervention strategy will be appropriate to address challenging behavior. If you don't yet know what's causing the behavior, tackling it may initially require some restraint. For some challenging behaviors, you may need to increase the severity of the intervention gradually. Always adopting a heavy-handed approach and applying a disproportionate amount of control over a group may desensitize them to the more direct actions, reducing their effectiveness over time.

Usually, a more subtle and gentle intervention can often be enough to address challenging behavior. Treating people like adults will encourage them to act like adults.

In this chapter, we will look at four gentle intervention strategies you can use when dealing with challenging behavior initially. They are gentle in their impact and subtle in their application. They will deal with the most common, minor, challenging behaviors experienced at events. If the behavior feels challenging, the gentle Green interventions can help to let the person know that you've noticed the behavior and are willing to address it. Even if your initial attempt doesn't work, the offender is on notice to expect more action if their behavior persists.

We will identify which challenging behaviors each intervention could realistically address. The intervention strategies covered in this chapter are:

1. Stealth mode
2. Use their name
3. Ask if they're okay
4. Move them around

1. Stealth mode

Stealth mode is one of the easiest and most minimal interventions you can do, but it requires some preparation of the room layout. The room layout should provide you with easy access to everyone. A cabaret layout works well here.

What challenging behavior suits this approach?

- Two participants chatting

- People with laptops and phones out who are not paying attention
- Participants who are nodding off to sleep
- Participants who are generally distracted

Stealth mode involves you casually moving towards the participant displaying the challenging behavior until you're standing next to or hovering behind them. While walking, you could be listening to a group discussion, presenting content, or observing an activity. The move towards the participant is casual. The aim is to look like you're connecting with the group in another part of the room. You should not be using a quick-step march with purpose.

Keep in mind the need to preserve psychological safety with the group.

Everyone in the room will be looking at you as you facilitate the event. As you move towards the offending participant, everyone's eyes will naturally follow. When you arrive at the offending participant (ideally behind them), that person will now be in the line of sight for the rest of the group. Everyone else will have to look past the participant to see you. To the person displaying the behavior, it will feel like they are now in the spotlight. Your presence, along with everyone's eyes now looking in their direction, can be enough to stop the behavior. Remember, keep in mind the need to preserve psychological safety with the group. The offending person should not feel intimidated by your presence, only aware.

TOP TIP

If you're using slides to present content, invest in a remote device that can move the slides along as well as hide the slides when needed. If you want everyone to be looking at you rather than the slides, being able to click the remote and hide the slide from wherever you are in the room compliments the subtle nature of Stealth mode.[19]

Stealth mode and discussions

If you're in the middle of running a learning discussion and not speaking, you can still deploy Stealth mode. Simply move towards the target participant and interject with a question or a quick summary. Again, this will draw everyone's attention to you and those around you.

Stealth mode and activities

If you're observing an activity, you can apply the same tactic as when running a discussion. You can ask the group about their progress from a position close to the offending participant, thereby drawing everyone's attention to you and them.

When you move away, the participant may well continue what they were doing. If so, simply step back and stay there for a more extended period. Eventually, they will get the message that you're aware of the behavior and would prefer it to stop.

Most participants appreciate the subtle nature of this intervention because they are not called out in front of their peers and made to feel like the "naughty child" of the group. They realize that by using the Stealth mode, you have noticed the behavior and will most likely escalate if it continues. That realization gives them a choice of stopping or risk an intervention escalation and potential embarrassment.

Remember, Stealth mode will only work if you have deliberately engineered the room layout to enable you to access everyone. If you can't access some of the participants, Stealth mode will not be possible, and other intervention strategies will be required.

2. Use their name

Remembering your participants' names is one of the critical skills to begin building a healthy working relationship with them. When someone wants to contribute, it's better to use their name rather than saying something like, "Yes, you in the blue shirt." If you don't know their name, ask them. If you have time, get hold of the participant list beforehand and do some research on LinkedIn or a similar networking tool. It will show you their faces and a profile of their background and skills.

Alternatively, get to know your participants (and their names) as they enter the room, as outlined in Chapter 5 – Engagement. Pay attention to names during introductions. I try to anchor each name by associating it with something I will remember.

Using alliteration is one way of doing this. For example, if someone called Tom talks a lot in their introduction, I will use alliteration to anchor his name - Talkative Tom. Bob may be wearing a brightly colored shirt. I would remember him as Bright Bob. Reinforce this by asking for a participant's name when they contribute to a discussion or ask a question. Name badges or tent cards on the tables can help you remember names too.

Remembering and using the names of those in your group does have a positive effect. I've often experienced participants coming up to me during a break and asking how I've managed to remember so many names. People are generally proud of their name. Taking the time and effort to remember names demonstrates that you care about your group and it shows that you respect them. Showing care and respect to your group in such a simple way can help you connect with the group and build relationships with them.

What challenging behavior suits this approach?

Use their name suits participants who:

- Seem to be distracted or are chattering
- Seem reluctant to speak
- Need a confidence boost
- Have raised objections or concerns

Getting the attention of those who are distracted

When trying to get someone's attention, ensure you use their name first, so they know a question is coming their way. They can then pay full attention to the request.

If you use their name last, after asking a question, it gives them less time to formulate an answer. Also, they may only hear their name and miss the request.

Catching someone out may embarrass them and result in them being more reluctant to contribute going forward. Using the name first works well if a participant is distracted or chatting because it gets their attention.

> *TOP TIP*
>
> *If you need support from your co-trainer, use their name to get their attention before asking them for help. They may be working on their next session or catching up with some work. Help your team to help you by getting their attention first and then asking them for the specific support.*

Engaging those who seem reluctant to speak

Some participants may be intimidated by other more vocal or senior participants in the room and therefore be reluctant to talk. They may need a confidence boost to affirm they belong in the room and can contribute. Encouraging them to join in by using their names can sometimes be enough for them to get over that intimidation. When they realize you know their name and are genuinely curious about what they have to say, they will often respond positively. Make sure you use their name first to let them know you're bringing them into the proceedings.

Boosting Confidence

If you know someone has expertise based on their introduction, you can legitimize your request. For example, "Karen, based on your introduction, it sounded like you're an expert on this topic. What do you think about this?"

You can also boost the confidence of those who don't speak very often by using their name to link back to what they said earlier. For example, "Linking back to the point that Jack made earlier about. . . ." If participants feel they have been seen and heard, their confidence will grow, and they're likely to contribute again. Linking back to a point made in earlier discussions increases the relevance and status of that point and boosts confidence.

Addressing objections

Using participant's names can also be useful to pace out future objections or challenges. For example, someone may have raised objections earlier in the event about a new change initiative. You can head off another complaint by referring to that participant and their previous objections; for example,

"Louise, earlier, you raised a concern about the time it will take to implement this new change. We're now going to talk about how we fund the change initiative. Would you have similar concerns here?"

Using Louise's name shows her that you have heard and understood her perspective. The aim is to surface the objection or challenge for Louise on her behalf. She doesn't have to embark on another time-consuming rant because you've already surfaced it for her. The example ends with a closed clarification question. All Louise has to say is yes or no.

Using the names of your participants is helpful when building relationships at the event. It helps to remind everyone that the room is full of individuals with feelings, hopes, dreams, and issues rather than a room full of employees with role titles. Using names will help people feel they belong in the room and feel valued. If people feel valued, they are less likely to display challenging behavior.

3. Ask if the person is okay

As with the Stealth mode, checking in with someone to see if they're okay can be subtle, yet effective, if done well. The first point to make with this intervention strategy is that you need to be genuinely concerned about the person when asking them if they're okay. Any hint of sarcasm or criticism, either in your facial expressions or tone of voice, will invite an adverse reaction in the person you're targeting the question to, and the situation may well deteriorate.

The second point to make is that this strategy works hand-in-hand with using someone's name.

What challenging behavior suits this approach?

Ask if they're okay suits participants who are:

- Generally distracted
- Chatting
- Displaying negative body language

Distracted Participants

You never know what's going on in the other person's world, so proceed with caution. In one of my workshops, I had one man continually checking his phone. I applied Stealth mode a few times to no effect. He kept checking his phone regularly, although each time he did, it was only for a moment. It didn't look like he was checking his emails or catching up with social media; it looked like he was waiting for something. It was proving distracting to him, to the people around him, and me as the facilitator.

I asked him if he was okay, "Kevin, I've noticed that you keep checking your phone regularly. Is everything okay?" It turned out that his wife was expecting a baby, and she was overdue. She was an hour away by car, and he was waiting for the call to let him know the baby was on the way. No one in the room could comprehend why he was in the workshop rather than with his wife. After everyone had congratulated Kevin, we quickly worked out how we could best help him manage the situation so he could focus. I did offer Kevin the chance to leave the workshop and go home, but he insisted on staying. (The simple solution was for Kevin to switch his phone from silent to loud, so if there were an incoming call or text, he would know about it).

A person may look distracted, but they are often thinking or reflecting on what's being discussed. Proceed with caution!

Two people chatting

In one of my Leadership Development workshops, two guys were always chatting. They looked focused, so I was curious as to what was going on. When I looked closer, one guy was talking more than the other. I managed to park my irritation and asked them politely if they were okay. I didn't call out the behavior; I didn't need to since both men were chatting at the time. Both men were Italian. While one had excellent English language skills, the other did not and needed in-the-moment translation from English into Italian. I hadn't realized. I offered to speak a little slower to make life easier for them. I also ensured they worked together on activities that required pairs so they could switch to Italian and have a break from always having to translate from English.

Should you call out the behavior or not?

There's nothing to stop you merely asking if someone is okay first without naming the behavior. It may be enough. If the behavior persists, you can then escalate by checking in with the person again, this time calling out the behavior. The intervention can be done in the group while the event is running. It can also be done on a one-to-one basis as a mild confronting intervention during a break if you deem it more appropriate.

If you don't refer to the behavior and merely ask, "Are you okay?" a person is more likely to respond in a positive but vague way—"Yes, I'm fine. Thanks." This vagueness gives little insight into what might be going on. The upside of this is that it's less invasive. You have let them know you've noticed something in their behavior that's not quite right. You've also spared them the embarrassment of calling out the behavior in front of the group.

By calling out the behavior when asking if they're okay, you are much more likely to get an insightful response. The downside is that calling out the behavior could embarrass the individual when done in front of the group. Mitigate any embarrassment by being sincere, moving closer to the individual, and lowering the volume of your voice. There's no need to make the intervention feel like an announcement to the group. Alternatively, discuss what you've observed on a 1:1 basis with them during a break.

Negative body language

A person may look disengaged, but unless you check, you won't know for sure. I've worked with many participants who seemed very unhappy. I was affected by this perception. I started to question my event design and my ability to help the group. It wasn't until I asked them if they were okay did the full picture emerge. Most people usually respond positively. They are often fully focused and have no clue that they look miserable. They're thinking about the problem at hand. Others are genuinely struggling with a personal issue and are grateful for the concern.

4. Move participants around

The final Green intervention of moving participants around can be used when minor challenging behavior is more prevalent amongst the group. Moving people around can disrupt any unhelpful group dynamics.

Moving people around can also be used positively. For example, spreading a small number of experts around the room to work with different groups can help balance the group's knowledge. Alternatively, you can cluster the experts together to work on a more advanced problem to prevent them from being bored.

What challenging behavior does this approach suit?

- Two participants are chatting
- Participants who are distracting others
- The trouble-table
- Two-speed groups
- The dominating experts

The chatters and distractors

Moving participants around can help disrupt pockets of challenging behavior occurring in pairs, trios, or table groups. If two people are always chatting with each other, it can help break it up and prevent them from distracting others around them. The same applies to participants who are generally causing distractions. The people on the receiving end can be too polite to say anything, so they tolerate it. Moving the distractor to sit near more forceful personalities who won't tolerate disruption can be a simple way of dealing with the problem.

The trouble-table

Using the move strategy is especially helpful when dealing with a trouble-table. That's the table where all the mischievous participants have congregated. This intervention strategy can work in any event, even in regular meetings where participants know each other. The aim is to disrupt the current group dynamic and create a more productive one.

Experts and two-speed groups

The reasons for moving people can vary. It can be to eliminate a negative disruption or to enhance group success. For example, there may be a topic on the agenda where a proportion of the group are experts, whereas others in the group are complete novices and need help to catch up. Spreading the experts to act as coaches to those who need help will harmonize the ability of the group overall to progress. If you don't spread out the experts, the group could be in danger of performing at two speeds. The novices could be left behind, and the experts clustered together could feel frustrated at the inability of others to keep up.

By spreading the experts amongst the group, their sense of importance and involvement in the group typically increases, and knowledge transfer increases, as well. The group can then all work at the same pace creating more harmony.

Who to move?

You can move individuals, a small number of people, or everyone. If you need to move one person, there must be somewhere for them to go. If not, two people will have to swap places at a minimum. Moving individuals can be tricky. The move singles out the disruptor and penalizes the innocent person swapping places with them. Both people may feel aggrieved at the move and cause further disruption.

If only one person is causing a problem, I typically disguise this by moving a few people. Only moving a few people can be enough to resolve pockets of challenging behavior or boost group performance. For instance, if there are new people on the team, and they are clustering together, moving them around to work with more experienced colleagues can help them feel part of the team.

There may be many other reasons for wanting to move most people. There could be a table full of mischievous participants who feed off each other's behavior or a pocket of quiet participants who don't like to talk or take the lead.

Moving everyone can help if the group dynamic isn't working. Perhaps there are tribes in the group who refuse to collaborate with others. Maybe everyone has clustered with only those they know and are reluctant to engage with others. The other reason for moving everyone is to ensure each sub-group has the same mix of expertise to work on a topic.

TOP TIP

Have a few spare seats dotted around the room to enable you to move any individual disruptors.

How to move people

Whatever the reason for moving, keep it simple. If you're moving individuals, simply move them to where you need them to be.

To get a small number of individuals to move, you can pick one person per table group (cabaret layout) or get every fourth person to move to the next empty seat (other arrangements). You can apply this approach if there are a limited number of experts or new people in the room.

Getting everyone to move requires more effort. If you're using a cabaret layout with table groups, get everyone to count off based on the number of tables in the room, and their number becomes their new table (assign a number to each table). For example, if six people are sitting at four tables, participants will count to four and start again. Only one or two of the original occupants will remain at their table. The rest will spread across the other tables.

If the room layout is a conference table, horseshoe, or theater, simply get every second person to get up and move along two empty spaces. Not one, but two empty spaces! Participants at the end of the row simply join the next row up (if Theater style) or go back to the other end (if horseshoe or conference table layout).

If you want to reset the group dynamic to optimize group performance, but don't know who the experts are, there is a quick and easy way to find out. Ask everyone to get into one line based on their experience ranging from zero (never heard of the topic) to ten (I wrote the book on it). Allow the participants to quickly validate their place in line with those either side of them. You can also check the ratings by picking random participants in line. Once verified, you then give each participant a new team number, one, two, three, four, one, two, three, four, working down the line. It's vital to start with the experts at the top of the line. Each team is guaranteed to get one of the top experts. Also, each team should end up with the same mix of expertise as the counting continues down the line to the end where the novices are.

TOP TIP

People usually don't like being moved, so to combat this, I always put a positive spin on the move. It helps to explain the rationale when moving people. If the move helps people succeed, I explain the benefits of it. If the movement is to address challenging behavior, I usually say the move is to help with networking and to get to know and work with new people.

All the Green intervention strategies are quick and easy to deploy, requiring minimum fuss while achieving a positive impact. If you fail to achieve the desired effect, move to the Amber strategies.

CHAPTER 16

AMBER INTERVENTION STRATEGIES

Get the group to help themselves

The Amber intervention strategies are fun to use because they take the focus away from you, the facilitator. Amber interventions can tackle similar behaviors to the "Green" ones. They can also address more challenging behaviors. There are two possibilities for using them:

1. You jump straight to Amber
2. Move up to Amber, having already tried the Green strategies. You now need to increase the effort to stop the behavior

AMBER INTERVENTION STRATEGIES

Unless the conduct is severe, it's best to avoid jumping straight to the Red strategies. It's worth trying the Amber ones. In this chapter, we will look at three Amber strategies. The intervention strategies covered in this chapter are:

1. Get them busy
2. Peer pressure
3. Tell a story

1. Get them busy

If you find yourself running an event alone, the intervention strategy of "get them busy" is a great option to employ. It gives you two benefits. You instantly recruit help while also dealing with challenging behavior. Getting participants busy can cover a wide range of challenging behaviors. They range from mild ones such as chatting to more challenging ones such as dealing with folks who dominate discussions. Getting someone to do something will break the cycle. If someone looks disengaged or about to fall asleep, get them up and busy doing something.

What challenging behaviors suits this approach?

Getting your group busy works well when participants:

- Are dominating the discussion
- Look disengaged
- Look like they're about to fall asleep
- Look distracted
- Are chatting

Getting them busy also works well to address groups who are generally tired and lacking energy.

How to Get them busy

Getting folks busy can break up most challenging behaviors. If people are disengaged, chatting, looking tired, or dominating, getting them busy will disrupt the behavior.

During events, there are many opportunities to get your group busy. For instance, if there is a discussion to run or an activity to debrief, there can be a need to capture key points coming from the group on a flip chart or two. Giving someone the job of scribing responses from the group will get them out of their chairs and into the spotlight at the front. Taking them away from their positions in the group will disrupt the challenging behavior. Using scribes can also speed up the capturing of the points. Your new volunteers will be scribing while you manage the group.

Recruiting volunteers is something to consider even if there isn't any challenging behavior, especially if you're flying solo since it may prevent challenging behavior from occurring. In the debriefing example, you would capture the points at a slower pace as you listen to responses and write them up with the scribes. The slow pace may invite challenging behavior as some of the group become frustrated with the slower pace caused by your attempt to multi-task. Other jobs to get your group busy include:

- Help distribute handouts
- Make them table team (or sub-group) leads for an activity
- Nominate them to report back on an activity (you need to tell them beforehand so they can pay attention during the activity)

- Time monitor for an activity
- Get them involved in role-plays

Whatever way you get them busy, make sure you do it respectfully and courteously to encourage willing compliance. Also, make it clear they are still able to contribute to the discussion or debrief; otherwise, they may feel excluded.

What if everyone needs to get busy?

The "graveyard shift" is the period right after lunch, so-called because the energy and enthusiasm levels of participants tend to dip. The result is a dead atmosphere. If everyone needs to get busy, you may need to modify your plan. For example, rather than having a discussion where everyone sits, switch to running a learning activity.

Activities which have lots of smaller sub-groups work well because they require everyone to get involved. So long as you get to the same outcome, it doesn't matter how you get there. The product will be the same; only the process changes.

> *TOP TIP*
>
> *In your event design, always have a Plan B to accommodate the need to inject more energy into the process. If the energy is low and there's no time for a break, getting everyone busy can be enough to break the group snooze.*

2. Peer Pressure

Peer pressure is about using the rest of the group to help manage challenging behavior. Peer pressure can be self-managed through the explicit agreement of the social contract or led by the facilitator. If a participant displays challenging behavior, they are more likely to listen and respond to their peers because of their relationship with their peers. It's also helpful to enable the group to self-manage behavior wherever possible to avoid playing the role of the police officer and the facilitator. Spending too much time policing challenging behavior can not only sap your energy and enthusiasm, but also consume time and delay progress.

What challenging behavior suits this approach?

Peer pressure can tackle any challenging behavior which can be self-policed by the group. It also works well with participants who:

- Try to derail the event or take it down a different path
- Have their agenda or crusade to follow
- Won't let go of the current topic

A self-managing group

Enabling the group to self-manage challenging behavior can be done using the social contract. When forming the agreement, it should be made clear that if any of the group spots behavior contrary to the contract, they are permitted to call it out respectfully and politely. Self-managing can work well if the group's leader is in the room so long as it's not the leader displaying the challenging behavior. If it is, you should step in and resolve with the leader using other interventions such as Stealth mode or Confront.

Any behaviors listed in the contract (good or bad) will be in scope for the self-managed group. Common ones I've seen included are:

AMBER INTERVENTION STRATEGIES

- Time management—Getting everyone back on time
- One person speaking—No one gets interrupted
- Active participation—Everyone takes a turn to present back
- Using devices—No devices needed during the event

You can also use the social contract when you see challenging behavior and re-validate it with the group. For example:

"I've noticed a few of you have been using your phones over the last ten minutes or so. The group agreed in the social contract that we would put our phones away so we could all focus on the event. Can I check with everyone that this is still the case?"

Circumstances can change during an event, so keeping the social contract flexible and adapting it to fit changes can be helpful. If challenging behavior becomes pervasive, use the social contract to re-validate what's acceptable. It can help manage that shift in behavior.

Avoiding derailment

Peer pressure can be useful when individuals are trying to derail your event. Derailment can occur in many forms and can occur at any time. It could be a deliberate attempt to stall progress and sabotage the event. Most likely, the derailment is simply someone wanting to make a point. Examples include participants who:

- Take a topic in a different direction
- Talk a lot without making a point
- Embark on their crusade, regardless of what topic is being discussed

- Won't let go of an item because they feel their issue still exists

If you choose to ignore these people and carry on, you will likely turn them into hostages. These individuals will no longer want to contribute since they feel excluded. They will direct their frustration at you since you ignored them and decided to carry on.

In either case, first, validate the need of the participant whom you perceive to be derailing. It is good to check that your assessment of the situation is accurate. If it is, you can announce the position to the rest of the group. For example, "Rather than move onto discussing next year's strategy, Mike wants to focus on this year's hiring challenges. What would the group like to do next?"

Peer pressure can be useful when individuals are trying to derail your event.

It's then up to the rest of the group to decide which way to go. If the group feels it's important enough, they will agree, and you will have to adjust the agenda to accommodate. More likely, the group will want to move on. The lone wolf will have to accept the pack consensus to move on and get back in line with the group.

If you get a mixed reaction where half of the group want to go off-topic or spend more time on a topic and the other half don't, it's a tough call. In my experience, it doesn't happen very often, but if it does, I try to park the derailment until the end of the event. Those who want to spend more time on a topic can do so at the end, and those who don't can leave early. When I do this, it's amazing how the number of participants wanting to spend more time on a topic suddenly dwindles. It wasn't that important, after all!

Ultimately, as a facilitator, your role is to help the group achieve the desired outcome. It's for them to judge where best to spend the time. Your experience may help advise the group on what's realistic and achievable, given the time they have.

Where possible, use the power of the group. Help the group help you!

3. Tell a Story

There is power in being able to tell a good story. As human beings, we grew up with stories, and we remember lessons learned through stories, whether they are our own or someone else's. Stories can have a massive impact on persuading and convincing others.

What challenging behavior does this approach suit?

- The reluctant or doubting participants who prefer the way things are now
- Participants who don't agree with a decision based only on logic
- Impatient participants who want to move faster than the rest of the group

The doubters and those who rely on their feelings

In some events where organizational transformation or personal change is required, there will be resistance from some participants who prefer the way things currently are. Simply telling them that they need to change won't work unless you have tremendous influence. Even then, they may not mentally buy into the change required.

However, telling a story about how other people and organizations have changed, the journey they took, and the successful outcome may be enough to begin to dissolve their resistance. The story may connect with them and their fears at an emotional level.

You can apply the same approach when trying to solve a problem with the group who may be resistant to the activity. Often, people don't fully appreciate the problem unless they have felt it. Some members of the group may not even acknowledge that the topic is a problem that needs addressing. Telling a story, from the perspective of an end-user or customer can invite empathy into a group who seems reluctant to tackle the problem. Merely telling the group they need to solve a problem that they think isn't important will be difficult. Inviting empathy using stories can move their position to one where they are motivated to solving the problem. You can only tell a story from someone else's perspective if you've done your research and can accurately represent their view. Alternatively, you could check to see who from the group could share the customer's story from their experience.

Logic versus feelings

If you have someone resistant to change, there is usually a reason behind it, and targeting their logical side of the brain won't be enough. Some people tend to make decisions based on feelings rather than logic.[20] The logic may be there, but to them, it simply doesn't feel right. Stories will help you to appeal to the participants' emotional side of the brain.

For example, when faced with someone who's resisting change at a personal level, I ask the group to think of someone they know who's gone through personal transformation. To build momentum and increase buy-in, I try to put people in small groups, and they take turns to share their stories. Most people can think of at least one person, either at home or at work.

The stories can be uplifting and can show the group two things. The stories show how pervasive personal change is and how frequent people succeed at personal transformation. Additionally, lessons from stories begin to seed the thought that change is possible for the participants.

The other benefit of getting the group to share stories is that it can strengthen the bond between the teller and their audience. Stories begin to reveal deeper insights into others and their lives. A deeper understanding and appreciation of each other can build empathy and engagement within the group.

I always have my own story of personal change ready in case the group asks. If asked, I share how I've reinvented myself as my career has progressed. I've been a Chartered Accountant, Management Consultant, Project Manager, Program Manager, Trainer, Facilitator, Certified Coach, and Author. Although each career transformation felt scary, the excitement of the new direction took over and helped me overcome any fear. The moral of the story is that at each stage, I've learned new skills that have opened a world of new opportunities. Those opportunities have kept life very interesting and have enabled me to continue to grow in my career.

If you tell a story about yourself, you are opening yourself to be vulnerable to the group. The groups often appreciate this. It gives permission for others in the group to do the same. To build on this, I would invite the group to share a similar story of their own.

It's hard to expect the group members to be open and share if you're not prepared to do it yourself, so you may have to go first. I keep my own stories in reserve and try to keep the focus on the group, not myself.

Getting the group to share stories begins to mix this strategy with a hint of peer pressure. Listening to how their peers have changed and succeeded within their organization can be the catalyst needed to shift the thinking of those who don't believe it's possible.

TOP TIP

When telling a story, make sure there is a learning point to it. It may be a great story, but does the story answer the "so what?" question. What's the purpose of the story? What's the learning from it which is relevant to the group? Help the group make the connection from the story to their specific situation. It will enable them to apply the learning to their context. Also, don't forget to include your emotions in the story; otherwise, it will simply be a list of facts.

You may not always have an appropriate story from your experience to share. In that case, think about what topics you're going to cover at the event and what other stories you can use. They could be from other people, from the news, or from other clients (so long as you protect names and specifics where appropriate).

Faster, Faster!

In the case of participants who want to move faster than the rest of the group and are beginning to get impatient, the classic Aesop's fable of the hare and the tortoise is often an excellent story to reference. There's an updated video version about the turtle and the rabbit published by Ramesh Cn, which builds on the classic fable.[21] It covers several stories, each with a different learning point. The final tale is about recognizing each other's strengths and working together to help everyone win. The tale shows that by helping each other, the team achieves a better result than if they were working alone and relying on their skills.

A current example that illustrates the same learning relates to graduate hiring in one of the large management consultancy companies. During their induction period, the

AMBER INTERVENTION STRATEGIES

recruits are given individual tasks to complete. However, when they complete their task, they cannot leave and go home until everyone has finished. The ones who finish first soon realize that helping those who are working at a slower pace can enable everyone to go home earlier. The inductees learn the lesson of teamwork trumps individual brilliance.

Avoid getting into a lengthy debate with the impatient participants about the speed and progress of the event. Instead, tell a short story that illustrates the power of working as a team. It's less confrontational and more likely to persuade the impatient participants to shift their perspective.

I've listed only two examples of how you can use stories to tackle challenging behavior. You can apply the same principle to almost any behavior. The learning within the story needs to relate to the current context to invite a change in behavior.

Telling stories to appeal to the emotional side of participants who object to something is another indirect way of tackling challenging behavior. You are not trying to convince the objector yourself. The story and its learning point will attempt to influence by connecting the learning to the current context and objection.

CHAPTER 17

RED INTERVENTION STRATEGIES

Danger, Danger!

Employing a Red strategy suggests there is an imminent danger to the event. Going through the thought process discussed in Chapter 14 will have determined that urgent and significant intervention is required. The consequences of leaving the behavior unchecked could harm the event and its progress. You may have already tried some of the Green and Amber strategies with little success. Now it's time to tackle the behavior head-on. A Red intervention should not come across as harsh to the receiver. The severity level implies more time, effort, and care will be needed to address the behavior. In this chapter, we will look at four Red intervention strategies that can tackle most of the challenging

RED INTERVENTION STRATEGIES

behaviors experienced at events. The intervention strategies covered in this chapter are:

1. Confront
2. Build relationships
3. Stage Management
4. Take a break or stop the event

1. Confront

Few people enjoy dealing with conflict and having difficult conversations. Most people would prefer to avoid such things for fear of making matters worse. When you confront somebody who's been displaying challenging behavior, do it with care and respect. No matter how irritated you may be, the goal is to protect the relationship and to increase the possibility of compliance. Telling someone off like a naughty child won't work. The response may be child-like, and the behavior is likely to persist out of spite.

Treating someone as an adult will encourage a positive reaction, which will help resolve the situation.

What challenging behavior does this approach suit?

- Any challenging behavior which is disruptive to the group
- Where previous intervention strategies have failed to have the desired impact

Confronting should not be the first intervention strategy applied. Ideally, you will have used other, more subtle interventions such as "Stealth mode" and "Asking if they're okay." It is tempting to go straight to confronting, but sometimes, it can feel unfairly harsh to those on the receiving end. Confronting is also time-consuming and often requires a break to find a suitable opportunity to talk to the target person.

General Confronting

Adopting helpful PREVENT mitigation strategies such as agreeing to a social contract can also help limit the need for confronting. Having an agreement to refer to can allow a gentle confrontation to be done in the group if appropriate. For example, "In our social contract, we agreed not to use cell phones during the session. Can you please refrain from using your cell phone until the break?" A general announcement can reaffirm the social contract if multiple participants are displaying challenging behavior.

Explore first

Before launching into a 1:1 confrontation, consider how much you know about the person and what drives their behavior. Understanding more about what's going on with someone may influence what you say. For example, rather than requesting they stop, you may ask them how they see the situation compared to you.

Participants often have no idea of their impact on others and are shocked when it's pointed out to them. If so, there's no need to make a request. They get it!

Others may get defensive, trying to justify their actions. You can choose the appropriate tone and level of the request based on the reaction of the participant.

> *TOP TIP*
>
> *When exploring, avoid using a "why" question since it often provokes a defensive answer and justification.*

RED INTERVENTION STRATEGIES

When someone is defensive, they are sensing a threat, which means their flight/fight response has kicked in, and they may no longer be receptive to any request you make. Asking other open questions using words like "what" and "how" will provoke explanation. The dialogue may provide you with new, helpful insights to make a more informed request in the 1:1 confront.

1:1 Confronting

If confronting is necessary and the behavior warrants a more sensitive approach, it is helpful to conduct a one-to-one basis in private to avoid embarrassment. Examples include those who:

- Dominate the event
- Look like they don't want to be there
- Are moaning and groaning about everything
- Seem insensitive to others' feelings

The list is endless. You'll have to make a judgment call based on how you see the behavior impacting the rest of the group, as discussed in Chapter 14. Ideally, confronting on 1:1 basis should be done during a break where the intervention is less evident. If a break is a long way off and the confrontation can't wait, taking the individual outside the room for a moment is an option or taking them to one side during a group activity. If you have a team, they can assist with the confront if available. Make sure you are all aligned with your team on the intervention required.

If nothing else has worked and you need to confront an individual on a 1:1 basis, it is best to follow the same thought process as covered in Chapter 14. Explaining the impact on you and the rest of the group may provide the person with another perspective. Using your observations to drive the intervention will help avoid using judgments and opinions. It's tough to dispute what has been seen or heard.

Example confronting intervention:

Call out the behavior: "I've noticed you have been interrupting other group members when they're trying to make a point. They're unable to finish making their point. You interrupted Tom on point x, Sally on point y, and Sam on point z."

Share the impact on you: "Your interruptions prevent me from understanding the views of others on key topics. I don't see the full picture from the group."

Share the impact on the group: "I've noticed that others are now speaking less and not contributing to the discussions."

Share any consequences: "I'm worried we will take key decisions without knowledge of all the facts and full buy-in from the group."

The request: "I would appreciate it if you would let others finish their point. Letting others speak will help everyone in the group feel involved and part of the decision-making process."

The request was very polite, beginning with "I would appreciate it if. . . ." The strength of the request may vary. The severity of the behavior, the personality of the person you're dealing with, and cultural norms are all factors to consider when deciding on the request strength.

Varying strength requests could be:

"I would appreciate it if . . . ."
"I would prefer it if . . . ."
"I need you to . . . ."
"I expect you to . . . ."
"I insist you do/don't do . . . ."

Operating at the firmer end of the spectrum may have more impact, but it may feel demeaning to the recipient. Tread carefully!

Multiple confronts

If the initial confronting request didn't work and the behavior persists, try again by increasing the request strength (I need, I expect, I insist). In extreme cases, offering the chance for the person to leave the event is an option.

2. Build a relationship

Building a relationship is a positive confronting intervention. The primary intent is to get to know the person displaying the challenging behavior. It is to understand them and learn what's driving their behavior. As described in Chapter 5, showing interest in a person will help build a relationship with them. The secondary intent is for the person to stop the behavior, having been listened to and understood. There's no guarantee that the behavior will end, but by being listened to, they may be more open to being influenced by you and your request.

What challenging behavior does this approach suit?

- When you're irritated with a person displaying challenging behavior

- Any prolonged challenging behavior
- Where previous intervention strategies have failed to have the desired impact

When you're irritated

Ideally, by being curious, not furious, you won't be irritated with anyone, but in case someone does aggravate you, building a relationship with them may help. The consequences of doing nothing is no change. The person will continue to annoy you. Your tolerance and patience with others may reduce because of your irritable mood.

If you're able to understand what's driving the behavior, there is a chance you will feel empathy for them and their situation. Having more compassion and less irritation will enable you to discuss the matter more objectively.

In one of my Customer Relationship Skills courses, I once had a participant who generally seemed very angry. Mike was very dismissive, moaning about the company and its processes and how everything seemed stacked against him. I'm a positive person, so Mike's constant negativity was beginning to wear me down.

> **The consequences of doing nothing is no change.**

Mike would regularly mutter and grumble quietly to himself when others would speak. Whenever I asked Mike if he was okay, he would use it as an opportunity to vent his frustration more vocally. The rest of the group didn't appreciate this. I noticed I was becoming more irritated because of the time consumed. Whenever I asked Mike what we could do about the situation he was complaining about, he simply shrugged his shoulders and would say, "Nothing we can do!"

No one else wanted to engage and join Mike in his desperate world, so we would park it and move on without resolving Mike's complaint.

Over a break, I decided to talk to Mike. As we queued for coffee, I simply asked him, "In class, you generally seem unhappy about a whole bunch of things. What's going on for you, and how can I help?"

With coffee in hand, he told me about the recent takeover of the company and how frustrated he was with the new ways of working. The processes had changed, the systems had changed, and it was all too much for him. He was managing a client project, and his team was bombarding him with questions about the new processes and systems. It was extra work for Mike. He was frustrated about the extra work, which was taking him away from his clients.

He told me he didn't want anything to be fixed. He knew it was a short-term issue. He simply wanted to share his frustration. I listened to what he had to say, played the key points back to Mike, and empathized with his situation. At the end of our chat, Mike looked relieved. I had taken the time to listen and understand Mike's perspective. He truly appreciated it. After the intervention, Mike's behavior improved. He seemed calmer and more optimistic when he spoke during group discussions. Showing genuine interest in someone can have a positive and immediate impact on them.

Prolonged behavior and previous failed attempts

If the challenging behavior persists and previous attempts at tackling have failed, it could be due to your irritation. The way you've tried to tackle the behavior before may have made things worse. The behavior remains unresolved, and your irritation has increased. Apart from ejecting the person from the event, the only way forward to diminish the irritation is to understand the person and what they may be struggling with.

Building a relationship can help you see beyond the behavior

As in the video "It's not about the nail," published by Jason Headley,[22] we often assume we know how to fix a problem based on what we are seeing. When we see someone behaving in a certain way, we focus on the behavior. However, this can be a symptom rather than the root cause. By listening to the other person and understanding their perspective and feelings, we naturally start to build a relationship with them. We can then begin to understand what's driving the behavior. The new clarity may lead to a very different intervention strategy.

TOP TIP

To build a relationship, changing the environment often helps. Sitting down over lunch may facilitate a more pleasant atmosphere to start a relationship-building conversation. If there's time, I find going for a short walk with a participant, even if it's merely to the coffee shop, can help. Both of you walking in the same direction, sharing the same vista, takes away the intensity of staring at each other. Going in the same direction, side-by-side with a participant can help. It says, "I'm with you, and I'm going your way." Warning–Know your limits! You're a facilitator, not a psychotherapist. Listening and building relationships will help in most cases, not all.

3. Stage Management

Stage Management is similar to Confronting in that the person displaying the behavior is confronted on a one-to-one basis privately during a break. If multiple people are trying to dominate the group, you can speak to them all at the same time.

What challenging behavior suits this approach?

Stage Management suits participants who:

- Are dominating discussions
- Consider themselves experts
- Are trying to take over the event
- Are trying to impress you and others in the room

Negotiate a separate agreement with dominating experts

Stage Management is about working with dominating experts to agree when and how they can actively join. For example, John may be dominating discussions and answering all the questions. Rather than continuing to allow John to dominate, we could agree that he won't say anything until invited. You need to honor the agreement and ask John for his input for this to work.

Stage Management acknowledges someone's expertise and controls how much of it is shared amongst the group. For example: "Manuel, your planning expertise on the next topic will be beneficial to the group. I will invite you to spend five minutes advising the group on their proposed plan. However, it would be helpful if you remain quiet while the group formulates their plan. Would that be okay?"

Stage Management requires negotiation skills. You want someone to modify their dominating behavior in return for guaranteed contributions. You're not shutting them down entirely. Shutting them down would potentially create a more challenging response from them. The dominators see themselves as helping the rest of the group, saving them from their ignorance on the topic. They would see any punitive action as unfair.

During the negotiation with the dominators, it can be helpful to point out the impact they're having on the rest of the group. While their intent may be to help the group, the effect may be very different. They may not be aware of it and having such awareness can be enough for them to want to modify their behavior. If not, it's worth remembering that in a negotiation, it's helpful to know your alternatives if you can't reach an agreement. Options could include asking the dominator to:

- Not to speak at all; or
- Leave the event because of their disruptive impact on the group

Faced with such choices, dominators will often accept a Stage Management request.

Combine Stage Management with Get Them Busy

Another way of stage-managing input from the dominators is to link Stage Management to the Get them busy intervention. Assigning them as coaches to a table team during activities is a way of channeling their enthusiasm in a targeted way. If they know they will be called upon to help and advise during exercises, they are more likely to tone down their input during discussions.

Tackling the takeover bid

If there's only one dominating expert who appears to be attempting a coup, the best way of tackling it is to embrace it. Going into battle with a usurper will harm the group. It will take time and focus away from the event objectives. It is preferable to keep the expert on your side to help the group. If the expert (and group) agrees, you can promote the usurper to become an observer and coach. They can help monitor activities and provide coaching to the group. Very often, the experts and dominators want to show everyone else how much of an expert they are. Giving them a managed opportunity to do so is usually enough to satisfy this need.

Are the Dominators real experts?

Stage management only works if the rest of the group recognize the individual(s) as experts. If someone is not an expert and their constant interruptions are nothing but noise which isn't helping anyone, Stage Management isn't the best option. People arriving late and feel they need to make up for lost ground by contributing to the event are good examples of non-value noise. If participants are not adding value when contributing, Confronting is often a better option than Stage Management.

4. Take a break or Stop the event

Taking an impromptu break or stopping an event to deal with challenging behavior is quite rare, but it does happen.

What challenging behavior suits this approach?

Stopping the event or taking a break can help when participants:

- Are out of control
- Are extremely emotional
- Are drunk or abusive to others
- Display threatening behavior towards others (and you)
- Feel the event is not moving in the right direction

The Emotional, out of control, rollercoaster.

Taking an impromptu break can help if emotions are running high amongst the group. It may help to take a break if everyone needs a chance to reset their emotional barometers. Taking an impromptu break can also be necessary when the group is out of control. Out of control groups are where a high proportion of participants are misbehaving. Other intervention strategies haven't worked, and the situation has gotten worse. Individually, the behaviors are irritating, but collectively, they cause significant disruption to the success of the event.

I've seen this happen during an event right after an organizational announcement, which signaled potential job losses. The news causes mixed emotions in the group, including anger, frustration, apathy, and resentment, making it hard for the group to achieve any progress. I've seen people throw things in frustration, kick furniture, swear, scream, and shout, all because of the pressure they're facing. Trying to carry on with the event straight away will be a waste of time. Giving folks a chance to vent with each other before attempting to restart can help.

> **Taking an impromptu break can help if emotions are running high amongst the group.**

Some topics during events or even whole events can cause emotions to run high, which can often require impromptu breaks. Team mediation sessions are a good example. Conflict exists either in the same team or between two groups. The event focuses on resolving the dispute and finding a way through. Emotions run very high in those events because each side feels that they occupy the high moral ground on the issue. Each side thinks the other is at fault, and they are blameless. If you believe the situation warrants everyone taking a breather, do so.

If there's not an official break scheduled and no refreshments available, still take a break and allow everyone to get some fresh air. Merely allowing everyone to get out of the room can often be enough for them to recover a sense of perspective on the topic. It will also allow emotions to settle down before engaging in the next item (or carrying on with the current topic). It's better to lose ten minutes or so and allow everyone to cool down than to push on to the next item. You will likely achieve nothing because of the emotional baggage being carried forward from the previous session.

Dealing with abusive and drunken behavior

For drunk individuals, who are offensive to others or displaying threatening behavior, this requires a delicate touch to avoid aggravating the situation. This situation has only ever happened to me once in twenty years. Such behavior is not acceptable in any case. What you do here will depend on the individual. For instance, in my situation, the workshop was scheduled for a whole day, but it had to be stopped right after lunch.

One person had drunk too much wine over lunch and told everyone what he thought about them and the "dumb" project he was tasked to lead. The group needed his input to critical decisions, and they were not going to get that. I called for an impromptu break to allow the rest of the clients some time to decide what they wanted to do. The clients rescheduled the workshop a week later.

Moving in the wrong direction

There can be times when most of the group feels the event is moving in the wrong direction. A great example has been where I ran a solutions workshop. There was disagreement amongst the group about which solution was the best. No one could agree on the decision-making criteria for the solution and had differing views on the problem too. We weren't making any progress and were going around in circles.

I asked for an impromptu break, which enabled me to gather the key stakeholders in the group and work out how to move forward.

It was futile trying to carry on with the workshop as it was because most people were not ready to listen to each other and work together. If you're running an event that seems to be going nowhere, you must address it.

Break or reschedule?

If a participant is not a vital member of the team, the show can go on without them. An impromptu break will allow you (or the sponsor) to deal with the situation. If it's a critical member of the group, rescheduling may be the better option.

Giving the group a choice of having a break to reset or rescheduling the event can often provide a group with a jolt, enough to halt pervasive behavior. If you have a break, be clear and get agreement on what you expect when the group returns. Update the social contract accordingly.

In extreme circumstances, you may need to reschedule the event. Buying time between events can help the group reflect on what went wrong and how to avoid similar mistakes in the future.

Whatever the situation you find yourself in, knowing that you can call on these interventions can be helpful.

> *TOP TIP*
>
> *When applying intervention strategies, be mindful of being as consistent as possible with members of the group. Treating one person more harshly than another when they're displaying the same behavior will seem unfair. Others in the group may also spot unfair treatment. Very soon, the mood and attitude of the group may deteriorate as a result.*

SUMMARY OF PART III

THE SWAN

There are eleven interventions within the three severity levels of Green, Amber, Red. Working through the thought process of three questions will buy you some buffer time between reaction and response to help you choose the right intervention. The three questions are:

1. How does the challenging behavior make me feel?
2. What might be going on with the individual displaying the behavior?
3. What's the impact on the group and the consequences of letting the behavior continue?

Going through these questions in real-time can take seconds. It will be valuable time spent as it will help determine an intervention which will:

- Stop the challenging behavior
- Protect the relationship
- Minimize disruption to the group

If the behavior is minor, the green strategies may be best to try first. Each intervention is subtle and requires minimal effort to deploy. The interventions are:

1. Stealth mode
2. Use their name
3. Ask if they're okay
4. Move them around

Amber strategies can help address behaviors that are pervasive or where there is general resistance in the group. They take the focus away from you, the facilitator and use the power of the group to tackle behavior. Each intervention will take more time and effort to deploy than the green ones, but they can address behavior at the individual or group level. The interventions are:

5. Get them busy
6. Peer pressure
7. Tell a story

Red strategies can help address most, if not all, behaviors because they require some form of confrontation. Going straight to this type of intervention first may seem heavy-handed if the behavior is minor. It is best to use red strategies when the behavior is disrupting the group and hindering progress. The impact on the receiving end of a red intervention should not feel harsh or unfair. Using your observations, tone of voice, and language choice when requesting a change in behavior can help generate the right impact. The interventions are:

8. Confront

9. Build a relationship

10. Stage Management

11. Take a break or stop the event

Knowing you have plenty of options at your disposal can help boost your confidence in handling any behavior that occurs and becoming a fearless facilitator. It will help you to focus on adding value to the group and helping them achieve success.

Remember. Most of the time, your group will be as wonderful as you are. The more effort, energy, and enthusiasm that you can bring to an event, the less likely you will encounter challenging behaviors.

EPILOGUE

The more I practice, the luckier I get.

~ Arnold Palmer

You don't go to the gym once and become fit. You don't become skilled at driving a car by just reading a manual. Learning a new skill and getting good at it takes time, effort, and resilience.

By reading this book, you have given yourself a massive advantage over other leaders. You now understand what it takes to lead successful events, and deal with difficult questions and behaviors. The skill of adding value through facilitation is not widely recognized. Creating a safe environment to guide a group through a process and reach a successful outcome can be incredibly helpful and valuable.

It has taken me twenty years to learn how to be a fearless facilitator. This book aims to cut that time down for you, drastically. How long do you think it will take you?

While this book has given you the tools and techniques to be successful in leading events, it will require practice to improve your skills. The more you practice and hone those skills, the easier it will feel to facilitate your way through any challenging situation.

I wish you every success and invite you to let me know how you get on at paul@paulmaltby.com.

NOTES

Chapter 2 - Resilience

(1) Carol S. Dweck. *Mindset: The New Psychology of Success: How We Can Learn To Fulfill Our Potential.* New York: Ballantine Books, 2006.

(2) Daniel Goleman & Richard J. Davidson. *Altered Traits: Science Reveals How Meditation Changes Your Mind, Brain, and Body.* New York, NY: Avery, an Imprint of Penguin Random House LLC, 2018.

(3) "The Three Minute Breathing Space Meditation Is Now Free To Download." July 27, 2011. http://franticworld.com/the-three-minute-breathing-space-meditation-is-now-free-to-download/

(4) "Free Meditations From Mindfulness For Health (You Are Not Your Pain)." http://franticworld.com/free-meditations-from-mindfulness/

(5) Rasmus Hougaard, Jacqueline Carter and Gitte Dybkjaer, "Spending 10 Minutes a Day on Mindfulness Subtly Changes the Way You React to Everything." April 27, 2017. https://hbr.org/2017/01/spending-10-minutes-a-day-on-mindfulness-subtly-changes-the-way-you-react-to-everything#:~:text=Decision making-,Spending 10 Minutes a Day on Mindfulness Subtly,Way You React to Everything&text=Leaders across the globe feel,more reactive and less proactive.&text=When practiced and applied, mindfulness,operating system of the mind.

(6) "How Much Sleep Do We Really Need?" June 1, 2020. https://www.sleepfoundation.org/articles/how-much-sleep-do-we-really-need

(7) Vicki Culpin. *The Business of Sleep: How Sleeping Can Transform Your Career.* London, UK: Bloomsbury Business, an Imprint of Bloomsbury Publishing Plc, 2018.

(8) "Caffeine and Sleep Problems." April 17, 2009. https://www.sleepfoundation.org/articles/caffeine-and-sleep

(9) "As We Get Parched, Cognition Can Sputter, Dehydration Study Says." https://www.newswise.com/articles/as-we-get-parched%2C-cognition-can-sputter%2C-dehydration-study-says

(10) "5 Brain-Boosting Chemicals Released During Exercise." March 24, 2019. https://cathe.com/5-brain-boosting-chemicals-released-during-exercise/

NOTES

(11) Ballantyne, Coco. "Does Exercise Really Make You Healthier?" January 2, 2009. https://www.scientificamerican.com/article/why-do-you-think-better-after-walk-exercise/

(12) Stephen Guise. *Mini-Habits: Smaller Habits, Bigger Results.* Middletown, DE: Createspace, 2013.

Chapter 3 - Environment

(13) Burnison, Gary, and Contributor. "7 Years Ago, Google Set Out To Find What Makes The 'Perfect' Team—And What They Found Shocked Other Researchers." September 13, 2019. https://www.cnbc.com/2019/02/28/what-google-learned-in-its-quest-to-build-the-perfect-team.html

(14) "At WD-40, We Call Our Employees Tribe Members." August 30, 2019. https://wd40careers.org/our-tribe

Chapter 4 - Venues

(15) Unit, Sustainable Design. "Natural Light in Learning Environments." https://www.academia.edu/2018655/Natural_light_in_learning_environments

(16) View. "Future Workplace Study: National Light and Air Quality Have the Biggest Impact on Workplace Wellness." https://view.com/blog/natural-light-workplace-wellness

Chapter 5 - Venues

(17) Susan RoAne, "How To Work A Room," YouTube Video, 2:06, March 5, 2011. https://www.youtube.com/watch?v=KtjMZpf60e4

Chapter 11 – Evolve the Question

(18) "George A. Miller: The Magical Number SevenPlus or Minus Two." https://www.all-about-psychology.com/george-a-miller.html

Chapter 15 – Green Intervention Strategies

(19) "Wireless Presenter with Red Laser: Wireless Presenter Remotes: Presentation Remote—Kensington." https://www.kensington.com/en-gb/p/products/control/wireless-presentation-remotes/wireless-presenter-with-red-laser/

Chapter 16 – Amber Intervention Strategies

(20) Jung, Carl G. *Psychological Types: A Revision.* Princeton, NJ: Princeton University Press, 1971.

(21) Ramesh, Cn, "Modern Teamwork Explained by The Rabbit and Turtle," YouTube Video, 5:37, January 25, 2012. https://www.youtube.com/watch?v=QWJgi4Pe3co

NOTES

Chapter 17 – Red Intervention Strategies

(22) Headley, Jason, "It's Not About The Nail," YouTube Video, 1:41, May 22, 2013. https://www.youtube.com/watch?v=-4EDhdAHrOg

INDEX

Accessibility, 53, 94
active listening, 139
addressing objections, 183
air quality, 53-54, 67
alcohol, 31, 35
alliteration, 181
amygdala, 24-25, 34, 169
ask them, 46, 181, 206
ask the group, 46, 135, 138, 148-149, 180, 200
ask if they're okay, 178, 185, 206
atrium, 50, 55
belief and confidence, 22, 26
beliefs, 169
blind spots, 107

brainstorming, 28
bucket, too difficult, 149
buffer, 168, 219
build relationships, 83, 181, 205, 209
Burgess, Keith, 106
caffeine, 31-32
celebrate success, 81
challenging history, 88, 90
clarify interest, 119, 121
climate thermometer, 46
cognition, 33
common ground, 70, 74-77, 95, 111
confidence in the design, 28
confidence by rehearsing, 28

confidence through visualizing success, 28
confidentiality, 41-42
conflicting values, 169
confront, 1:1, 207
creeping death, 77
crusade, 125, 196-197
curious not furious, 170-171, 210
Davidson, Richard J., 24
debrief, 80, 194-195
derailment, 91, 97, 197-198
desired outcome, 13-14, 16, 94, 109, 116, 198
Dweck, Carol, 23
ELMO, 153-155, 157
energy in the room, 45, 70, 108
energy boost, 105
energy levels, 32, 35
Erasmus, Desiderius, 109
exercise, 32
experts, 52, 59, 96, 187-191, 213-215
facilitation style, 105, 107
fearless, 4, 21-23, 29, 221, 224
feedback, 100, 102-103, 112
feeling threatened, 48, 169
flight or fight, 24-25, 48, 82, 92, 169, 207
Ford, Henry, 26
Funnel, 130-131, 138
get them busy, 193-195, 214, 220

Goleman, Daniel, 24
graveyard shift, 195
growth mindset, 23-24, 110, 117
Guise, Stephen, 33
hangover, 29, 31, 35
Headley, Jason, 212
high energy, 63, 74, 105
Hougaard, Rasmus, 25
hydration, 32
icebreaker, 74-76, 90
ideal future, 148
impromptu break, 153-154, 166, 215-218
informal hierarchies, 17
influencer of climate, 44
intragroup dynamic, 139
introductions, 76-77, 181
jerk, 163, 172
knee-jerk reactions, 168
layout
   cabaret, 54, 57-59, 178, 190
   conference room, 61-63, 66
   u-shaped conference room, 59-61
   u-shaped chairs only, 63-65
lead facilitator, 106
listen and learn, 135, 137, 139
logic, 199-200
low energy, 35, 105
mad, sad, glad, 46

INDEX

managing expectations, 15
Miller, George A., 141
mindfulness, 24-25, 34
mindset of curiosity, 171
mini habits, 33
monotone, 164, 174
move them around, 178, 190, 220
multiple confronts, 209
Mural, 12
nail, 212
National Sleep Foundation, 30-31
natural light, 53, 66-67
negative boy language, 185, 187
negative feelings, 169
nerves, 23, 28
objections, 182-183
Palmer, Arnold, 223
panic, 24-25, 34, 77, 130
parking lot, 150-151
pause, breathe, think, 123
peer pressure, 155, 157, 193, 195-198, 201, 220
plan B, 28, 195
positive energy, 72
Potential Project, 25
prefrontal cortex, 24-25, 169, 174
previous events, 88-89
pre-work, 87, 92, 95-97, 111
priming, 87, 91-93, 111
problem solving, 13

Project Aristotle (Google), 41
psychological safety, 16, 41-42, 48, 70, 131, 179
purpose
    agreed, 14
    and outcome, 12-15, 18-19, 109
question
    clarification, 115, 129, 184
    closed, 126
    open, 126, 129, 207
real play, 79
relevance, 78-79, 97, 183
reset energy, 154
resilience
    mental, 22, 30, 34
    physical, 29-30, 35, 70
resourcefulness, 24, 125
Ridge, Gerry, 41
RoAne, Susan, 72
roleplay, 79-80
rollercoaster, 216
room
    breakout, 47, 51, 94
    main, 50-51, 67
    is too big, 55-56
    is too small, 54, 67
Rudman, Richard, 37
self-managing group, 196
sensitive topics, 88, 91
scribe, 103, 141-142
shift energy, 146
silence, 43, 129-31, 138, 147

Slack, 12
sleep, 31-32, 35
so what? 142, 144, 202
social contract
boundaries, 40, 110
create, 39
honor, 47
psychological safety, 41-42, 131
stage fright, 34
stage management, 205, 212-215
stealth mode, 178-180, 184-185, 196, 205, 220
summarize, 129, 135, 137, 139-142, 157
TALKS, 135, 137, 144, 149
target, 135-138, 140
team dynamics, 90
tell a story, 193, 199-201, 220
themes, 135-138, 141-144, 157
topic
sensitive topics, 88, 91
    topic champions, 59
    & pre-work, 95-95
    & TALKS, 135-138, 141
Trello, 12
trouble-table, 188
two-speed groups, 188-189
unhelpful feelings, 168
use their name, 178, 181-183
Venn diagram, 75-76
venue
    external versus internal, 52
    location, 49-50
    size, 54
well-intentioned, 172
what's in it for me? 78
water, 32
WD-40, 41
work the room, 71

ABOUT THE AUTHOR

Paul Maltby is the Professional Development Leader for IBM Services covering Europe, Middle East, and Africa. In his role, he and his team develop IBM's talent at all levels ranging from associates to senior executives. He is a conference speaker, facilitator, coach, and author.

As a management consultant, Paul addressed his fear of public speaking by becoming an internal trainer and facilitator. The training role sparked a passion for helping others to develop their skills and careers. That passion continues today. Over the last twenty years, Paul has facilitated hundreds of events reaching over 10,000 people.

As a learning specialist, Paul has designed, developed, and facilitated successful consulting and leadership programs worldwide, both face-to-face and virtually. He believes in continuous growth, which has led him to be a certified speaker and facilitator with the John Maxwell Team, an approved ProReal coach, and a licensed facilitator with the Arbinger Institute.

His favorite event is the 'Train-the-Trainer' course, which helps leaders and aspiring trainers to succeed in developing others. Whatever happens in that course can be turned into a learning opportunity.

He is married to Emma and has two children, Thomas and Poppy, who help him maintain a healthy perspective on life, and remind him his jokes are not that funny.

Your Next Steps with
The Fearless Facilitator

 **JOIN THE CONVERSATION:**
Share your own experiences

 **CATCH A FREE WEBINAR:**
Learn the latest Fearless tips and techniques

 **REQUEST COACHING:**
Find the support you're looking for

paul@paulmaltby.com

  thefearlessfacilitator

Coming next…
The Virtual Fearless Facilitator

- DEVELOP YOUR VIRTUAL PRESENCE AND ENGAGEMENT

- DESIGN AND DELIVER INTERACTIVE VIRTUAL EXPERIENCES

- INCREASE YOUR IMPACT WITH OTHERS

- MAKE VIRTUAL EVENTS SUCCEED FOR YOU AND YOUR TEAM

Can't wait? Feel free to contact me:

paul@paulmaltby.com

www.ingramcontent.com/pod-product-compliance
Lightning Source LLC
LaVergne TN
LVHW011813060526
838200LV00053B/3761